A BALANCED MATHEMATICS PROGRAM INTEGRATING SCIENCE AND LANGUAGE ARTS

Unit Resource Guide
Unit 6
Geometry

THIRD EDITION

KENDALL/HUNT PUBLISHING COMPANY
4050 Westmark Drive   Dubuque, Iowa 52002

A TIMS® Curriculum
University of Illinois at Chicago

UIC The University of Illinois at Chicago

The original edition was based on work supported by the National Science Foundation under grant No. MDR 9050226 and the University of Illinois at Chicago. Any opinions, findings, and conclusions or recommendations expressed in this publication are those of the author(s) and do not necessarily reflect the views of the granting agencies.

ISBN 978-0-7575-3621-2

Printed in the United States of America

1 2 3 4 5 6 7 8 9 10 11 10 09 08 07

Letter Home

Geometry

Date: _____

Dear Family Member:

In this unit students measure, build, analyze, and classify geometric shapes. They will focus on properties of geometric shapes and look closely at the angles and the sides. As we explore the attributes of shapes, your child will learn to communicate about geometry.

Help your child think about geometry by asking him or her to name geometric objects at home. Ask your child to identify the edges and corners of these shapes. Perhaps you or a relative or friend has an interest in quilts or other art forms that involve geometry. Discuss these interests with your child.

Continue to review the multiplication and division facts with your child. Use the *Triangle Flash Cards* for the last six facts (4×6, 4×7, 4×8, 6×7, 6×8, 7×8) to help your child practice these multiplication facts and the related division facts.

Sincerely,

_____

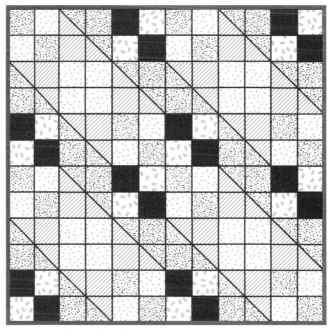

A quilt with many geometric patterns

Carta al hogar

Geometría

Fecha: _____

Estimado miembro de familia:

En esta unidad, los estudiantes medirán, construirán, analizarán y clasificarán figuras geométricas. Los estudiantes se concentrarán en las propiedades de las figuras geométricas y estudiarán detenidamente los ángulos y los lados. A medida que exploremos los atributos de las figuras, su hijo/a aprenderá a comunicarse acerca de la geometría.

Usted puede ayudar a su hijo/a a pensar acerca de la geometría pidiéndole que nombre objetos geométricos en casa. Pídale a su hijo/a que identifique los bordes y las esquinas de estas figuras.

Quizá usted o un familiar o amigo tenga interés en colchas u otra forma de expresión artística que use la geometría. Platique acerca de sus intereses con su hijo/a.

Continúe repasando las tablas de multiplicación y división con su hijo/a. Use las *tarjetas triangulares* de las últimas seis tablas (4 × 6, 4 × 7, 4 × 8, 6 × 7, 6 × 8, 7 × 8) para ayudar a su hijo/a practicar estos conceptos y los conceptos relacionados de división.

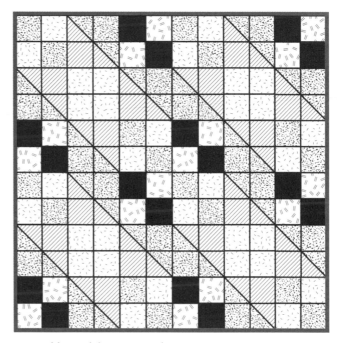

Una colcha con muchos patrones geométricos

Atentamente,

_____

Table of Contents

Unit 6
Geometry

Unit 6

Outline
Geometry

Unit Summary

Estimated Class Sessions
9-15

Students investigate patterns and concepts in geometry. They draw triangles and other plane figures and discover properties of the shapes. Students discover the relationship between the number of sides of a polygon and the sum of its angles. They describe and classify shapes. Tessellations are explored using quilt designs.

This unit contains a short assessment, *Making Shapes,* in which students draw shapes with specific properties and measurements. To complete the assessment, they use the *Telling* Rubric to guide their writing as they explain the strategies they used to draw the shapes.

The DPP for this unit reviews the last six multiplication facts (4×6, 4×7, 4×8, 6×7, 6×8, and 7×8) and the related division facts.

Major Concept Focus

- estimating angle measures
- multiplication and division facts: last six facts
- acute, obtuse, right, and straight angles
- similarity
- congruence
- tessellations
- naming polygons
- sums of angles in polygons
- properties of triangles and polygons
- triangulation
- measuring angles with a protractor
- classifying shapes
- drawing angles and shapes
- Student Rubric: *Telling*
- communicating solution strategies

Pacing Suggestions

This unit is designed to be completed in 9–15 days. Students' previous experience with the unit's geometric concepts, as well as the extent of students' explorations in each lesson, will determine how quickly the class completes the unit.

- The unit includes one optional lesson, Lesson 5 *Quilts and Tessellations,* which is an engaging investigation involving geometric patterns and reasoning. The lesson also provides many opportunities for connections to other subjects. Students can complete this lesson in conjunction with art or social studies classes, or individual students can work on it as an enrichment activity.

Assessment Indicators

Use the following Assessment Indicators and the *Observational Assessment Record* that follows the Background section in this unit to assess students on key ideas.

A1. Can students measure angles?

A2. Can students draw shapes and angles with given measures?

A3. Can students identify and describe 2-dimensional shapes?

A4. Can students classify 2-dimensional shapes?

A5. Can students identify congruent and similar shapes?

A6. Can students make and test conjectures about geometric properties?

A7. Can students use geometric concepts and skills to solve problems?

A8. Can students use numerical variables?

A9. Do students demonstrate fluency with the last six multiplication and division facts $(4 \times 6, 4 \times 7, 4 \times 8, 6 \times 7, 6 \times 8, 7 \times 8)$?

Unit Planner

	Lesson Information	Supplies	Copies/Transparencies
Lesson I **Angle Measures** URG Pages 27–41 SG Pages 184–191 DAB Pages 87–88 DPP A–D HP Part 1 *Estimated Class Sessions* **2**	**Activity** Students review benchmark angles (90°, 180°, 270°). They measure and draw angles with protractors. **Math Facts** Complete DPP items B and D for this lesson. Task B begins the review of the last six facts, while Challenge D uses operations to solve puzzles. **Homework** 1. Students complete homework *Questions 1–5* in the *Student Guide* after Part 1. 2. Students complete homework *Questions 6–8* in the *Student Guide* after Part 2. 3. Assign Part 1 of the Home Practice. Students use flash cards to review the last six facts. **Assessment** 1. Use *Question 8* in the Homework section in the *Student Guide* as an assessment. 2. Use the *Observational Assessment Record* to note students' abilities to measure angles.	• 1 protractor per student and 1 for the teacher • cardboard corners, optional	• 1 transparency of *Measuring Angles* DAB Pages 87–88, optional • 1 copy of *Observational Assessment Record* URG Pages 11–12 to be used throughout this unit
Lesson 2 **Angles in Triangles and Other Polygons** URG Pages 42–57 SG Pages 192–196 DAB Pages 89–90 DPP E–H HP Parts 2–3 *Estimated Class Sessions* **2**	**Activity** Students measure angles in polygons and discover that the sum of a triangle's interior angles is always 180 degrees. **Math Facts** Complete DPP items E and G. Item E provides practice with the last six facts. Item G introduces fact families. **Homework** 1. Assign *Questions 1–6* in the Homework section of the *Student Guide* after Part 1. 2. Assign *Questions 7–9* in the Homework section after Part 2. 3. Assign Parts 2 and 3 of the Home Practice. **Assessment** 1. Use DPP item M as an assessment. 2. Use the *Observational Assessment Record* to document students' abilities to identify, describe, and classify 2D shapes.	• 1 protractor per student and 1 for the teacher • 1 ruler per student and 1 for the teacher • 1 set of pattern blocks (6 green triangles and at least 1 of each of the following: yellow hexagon, red trapezoid, blue rhombus, brown trapezoid, purple triangle, tan rhombus, and orange square) per student group • 1 pair of scissors per student • 2 blank unlined sheets of paper per student • cardboard corners or plastic right triangle, optional • pattern block templates, optional • overhead pattern blocks, optional • large blackboard protractor, optional	• 1 transparency of *Measuring Pattern Block Angles* DAB Pages 89–90, optional • 1 transparency of *Regular Polygons* URG Page 52

	Lesson Information	Supplies	Copies/Transparencies
Lesson 3 **Polygon Angles** URG Pages 58–69 SG Pages 197–200 DAB Page 91 DPP I–J HP Part 4 *Estimated Class Sessions* **1-2**	**Activity** Students investigate the sum of the interior angles of various polygons to find patterns. **Homework** 1. Students can complete the homework problems in the *Polygon Angles* Activity Pages in the *Student Guide* after completing the *Polygon Angles Data Table.* 2. Assign Part 4 of the Home Practice. **Assessment** Use the Journal Prompt as an assessment.	• 1 calculator per student • 1 protractor per student and 1 for the teacher • 1 ruler per student	• 1 transparency of *Polygon Angles Data Table* DAB Page 91, optional
Lesson 4 **Congruent Shapes** URG Pages 70–81 SG Pages 201–204 DPP K–L HP Part 6 *Estimated Class Sessions* **1**	**Activity** Students explore properties of triangles. They investigate the difference between congruence and similarity. **Math Facts** Complete DPP item K for this lesson. **Homework** 1. Assign the Homework section in the *Student Guide.* 2. Assign Part 6 of the Home Practice. **Assessment** 1. Use DPP Task L Drawing Shapes as a quiz. 2. Use the *Observational Assessment Record* to document students' abilities to identify congruent and similar shapes.	• 10 straws plus extras per student group and 10 for the teacher • 4 chenille sticks plus extras per student group and 4 cut into approximately 5-cm lengths for the teacher • 1 pair of scissors per student • 1 centimeter ruler per student • 1 protractor per student	• 1 transparency of *Congruent Shapes Examples* URG Page 78 • 1 transparency of *A Triangle* URG Page 79 • 1 transparency of *Congruent Shapes* SG Pages 201–202, optional
Lesson 5 **Quilts and Tessellations** URG Pages 82–96 SG Pages 205–209 *Estimated Class Sessions* **3**	OPTIONAL LESSON **Optional Activity** Students analyze the geometry of quilt patterns and investigate tessellations. **Homework** Students complete the homework questions on the *Quilts and Tessellations* Activity Pages in the *Student Guide.* **Assessment** Use homework *Questions 1–2* as an assessment.	• 1 set of pattern blocks (12 green triangles, 12 orange squares, 3 yellow hexagons, 6 red trapezoids, 6 blue rhombuses, 12 tan rhombuses) per student group • 1 protractor per student and 1 for the teacher • plain unlined paper, optional • overhead pattern blocks, optional	• 3 copies of *Triangle Grid Paper* URG Page 94 per student plus extras, optional • 1 transparency of *Jacob's Ladder Quilt* URG Page 89 • 1 transparency of *Detail View of Jacob's Ladder Quilt* URG Page 90 • 1 transparency of *Four Quilt Patterns* URG Pages 91–92 • 1 transparency of *Regular Hexagons* URG Page 93

(Continued)

	Lesson Information	Supplies	Copies/Transparencies
Lesson 6 **Classifying Shapes** URG Pages 97–112 SG Pages 210–217 DAB Page 93 DPP M–P HP Part 7 *Estimated Class Sessions* **2-3**	**Activity** Students compare classifications in science to classifying polygons. **Math Facts** Complete DPP items O–P for this lesson. **Homework** 1. Assign the Homework section in the *Student Guide* before Part 2. 2. Assign Part 7 of the Home Practice. **Assessment** You can use The Flatville Zoo section in the *Student Guide* as an assessment.	• large art paper • glue • 1 pair of scissors per student • dictionary	• 1 transparency of *Classifying Shapes* SG Pages 210 & 212, optional
Lesson 7 **Making Shapes** URG Pages 113–123 SG Pages 218–219 DPP Q–R HP Part 5 *Estimated Class Sessions* **1-2**	**Assessment Activity** Students draw two-dimensional shapes based on information on an "order" for a slab of stone. **Math Facts** Complete DPP item Q, which quizzes the last six facts. **Homework** 1. Use uncompleted orders on the *Making Shapes* Activity Pages as homework. 2. Assign Part 5 of the Home Practice. **Assessment** 1. Use the *Slab Orders* Assessment Page to assess students' understanding. Score **Question 4** on the *Telling* Rubric. 2. Transfer appropriate documentation from the Unit 6 *Observational Assessment Record* to students' *Individual Assessment Record Sheets*.	• 1 protractor per student and 1 for the teacher • 1 ruler per student • straws and chenille sticks, optional • overhead ruler	• 1 copy of *Slab Orders* URG Page 120 per student • 1 copy of *TIMS Multidimensional Rubric* TIG, Assessment section • 1 copy of *Individual Assessment Record Sheet* TIG Assessment section per student, previously copied for use throughout the year • 1 transparency or poster of Student Rubric: *Telling* TIG, Assessment section

Preparing for Upcoming Lessons

Collect pennies and nickels for Unit 7 Lessons 7–8.

Connections

A current list of literature and software connections is available at *www.mathtrailblazers.com*. You can also find information on connections in the *Teacher Implementation Guide* Literature List and Software List sections.

Literature Connections

Suggested Titles

- Ellis, Julie. *What's Your Angle Pythagoras? A Math Adventure.* Charlesbridge Publishing, Watertown, MA, 2004.

- Friedman, Aileen. *A Cloak for the Dreamer.* Scholastic, New York, 1994. (Lesson 5)

- Hopkinson, Deborah. *Sweet Clara and the Freedom Quilt.* Paintings by James Ransome. Alfred A. Knopf, New York, 1993. (Lesson 5)

- Kinsey-Warnock, Natalie. *The Canada Geese Quilt.* Illustrated by Leslie W. Bowman. Cobblehill Books/Dutton, New York, 1989. (Lesson 5)

- Paul, Ann Whitford. *The Seasons Sewn: A Year in Patchwork.* Harcourt Brace & Co., New York, 1996. (Lesson 5)

- ————. *Eight Hands Round A Patchwork Alphabet.* Illustrated by Jeanette Winter. Harper Collins, New York, 1991. (Lesson 5)

- Ross, Catherine Sheldrick. *Squares: Shapes in Math, Science and Nature.* Kids Can Press, Ltd., Tonawanda, NY, 1996.

Software Connections

- *Building Perspective Deluxe* develops spatial reasoning and visual thinking in three dimensions.

- *The Factory Deluxe* promotes spatial reasoning and practices finding area.

- *The Geometer's Sketchpad* allows students to construct 2-dimensional figures and explore their attributes.

- *Math Arena* is a collection of math activities that reinforces many math concepts.

- *Math Munchers Deluxe* provides practice in basic facts and finding equivalent fractions, decimals, percents, ratios, angles and identifying geometric shapes, factors and multiples in an arcade-like game.

- *Mighty Math Number Heroes* poses short answer questions about fractions, number operations, polygons, and probability.

- *National Library of Virtual Manipulatives* website (http://matti.usu.edu) allows students to work with manipulatives including geoboards, base-ten pieces, the abacus, and many others.

- *Shape Up!* provides activities with five different sets of shapes.

- *Tessellation Exploration* provides opportunities to explore geometric concepts (flips, turns, slides) and to investigate tessellations. (Lesson 4)

- *Zoombinis Logical Journey* develops thinking skills as students find patterns to solve puzzles.

Teaching All Math Trailblazers Students

Math Trailblazers® lessons are designed for students with a wide range of abilities. The lessons are flexible and do not require significant adaptation for diverse learning styles or academic levels. However, when needed, lessons can be tailored to allow students to engage their abilities to the greatest extent possible while building knowledge and skills.

To assist you in meeting the needs of all students in your classroom, this section contains information about some of the features in the curriculum that allow all students access to mathematics. For additional information, see the Teaching the *Math Trailblazers* Student: Meeting Individual Needs section in the *Teacher Implementation Guide*.

Differentiation Opportunities in this Unit

Journal Prompts

Journal prompts provide opportunities for students to explain and reflect on mathematical problems. They can help both students who need practice explaining their ideas and students who benefit from answering higher order questions. Students with various learning styles can express themselves using pictures, words, and sentences. Teachers can alter journal prompts to suit students' ability levels. The following lessons contain a journal prompt:

- Lesson 3 *Polygon Angles*
- Lesson 5 *Quilts and Tessellations*
- Lesson 7 *Making Shapes*

DPP Challenges

DPP Challenges are items from the Daily Practice and Problems that usually take more than fifteen minutes to complete. These problems are more thought-provoking and can be used to stretch students' problem-solving skills. The following lessons have DPP Challenges in them:

- DPP Challenge D from Lesson 1 *Angle Measures*
- DPP Challenge J from Lesson 3 *Polygon Angles*
- DPP Challenge P from Lesson 6 *Classifying Shapes*
- DPP Challenge R from Lesson 7 *Making Shapes*

Extensions

Use extensions to enrich lessons. Many extensions provide opportunities to further involve or challenge students of all abilities. Take a moment to review the extensions prior to beginning this unit. Some extensions may require additional preparation and planning. The following lessons contain extensions:

- Lesson 1 *Angle Measures*
- Lesson 3 *Polygon Angles*
- Lesson 5 *Quilts and Tessellations*
- Lesson 6 *Classifying Shapes*
- Lesson 7 *Making Shapes*

Background
Geometry

One of the first schools was built in Greece, outside Athens in the 4th century BCE. The philosopher and mathematician Plato was the founder and teacher of this school. His school was in a grove of acacia trees belonging to a man named Academus. Hence, his school became known as the Academy, and the word *academy* still means a place of learning. Engraved atop the doorway was the school's motto, "Let no man ignorant of geometry enter here."

Our curriculum echoes Plato's belief that geometry is an important subject that deserves significant attention in the mathematics class. In this first geometry unit of fifth grade, students discover many important patterns and concepts of geometry. They construct triangles and other plane figures. Later in the unit, students can study and build tessellations in an optional activity. Activities that require children to build shapes focus their attention on the attributes or characteristics of the shapes they are constructing. This helps children advance in their geometric development.

Van Hiele Levels of Geometric Development

Mathematics educators in the United States are becoming increasingly aware of the insights of the Dutch educators Pierre van Hiele and Dina van Hiele-Geldof in the area of geometry education. Indeed, studies confirm the five levels of geometric development that the van Hieles described in the 1950s (Burger and Shaughnessy, 1986). The five levels are:

Level 0: Visualization. Students view geometric objects holistically. They can identify objects by their appearance, but not by attributes. For example, a student can identify a rectangle, but does not recognize that a rectangle has opposite sides equal and parallel.

Level 1: Analysis. Students begin to analyze the properties of objects. They are able to focus on their characteristics. For example, all sides of squares are equal and opposite sides of a parallelogram are parallel.

Level 2: Informal Deduction. Students use their understanding of properties to make simple deductions. They see relationships among figures. For example, a square has all the properties of a rectangle; therefore, a square is a rectangle.

Level 3: Deduction. Students write formal proofs based on an axiomatic system. A rigorous high school geometry course is taught at level 3.

Level 4: Rigor. Students can work with different axiomatic systems. This level corresponds to college work in geometry (Crowley, 1987).

The van Hieles found that each level, while not age-specific, builds on the previous level. Students proceed from level to level sequentially and no level can be omitted. They believed that advancement depends on content and method of instruction (Crowley, 1987).

A student's experiences in geometry at the elementary school level appear to be critical to success in later schooling. Research shows that those students who are at level 0 or 1 when entering high school geometry have a very poor chance of success. Students who begin high school geometry at level 2 have at least a 50% chance at succeeding (Senk, 1989). Unfortunately, many upper elementary students are at level 0. This is not surprising, as researchers found that most geometry questions asked in standard elementary math textbooks were answerable with level 0 understanding (Fuys, Geddes, and Tischler, 1988).

In *Math Trailblazers,* we introduce topics and concepts so children process new ideas over long periods of time, gradually building a solid foundation in mathematics. In this unit, we review level 0 ideas by asking students to identify and draw various polygons. Most of the work in this unit is at level 1. Level 2 ideas are introduced in an exercise in classification. Classification builds on the idea of inclusion. For example, since a square is a quadrilateral with four right angles, a square is a rectangle.

Some of your students may not comprehend the concept of inclusion at the end of this unit. Exposing them to the ideas of inclusion will help them develop understanding gradually. Mastery is not required at this time. You might talk about class inclusion with nonmathematical examples. The *Student Guide* discusses class inclusion with regard to classification of living things. Another example for children to think about is where they live. If you live in Milwaukee, then you live in Wisconsin, since Milwaukee is in Wisconsin. This idea can be taken further. Wisconsin is in the United States, and the United States is in North America, and so on.

Geometry and art are explored in an optional lesson on quilt patterns. Students analyze the geometry they see in quilts. They make their own patterns and discuss tessellations. This lesson develops van Hiele level 1 thinking. Children reason why certain polygons fit together while other polygons do not tessellate. You can expand this lesson and combine it with art class. You may know of an expert on quilts who would be willing to talk to your class. Also, you can investigate Islamic and Moorish art that contains many interesting geometric patterns. Many students find the work of M.C. Escher to be fascinating. Unit 10 includes a lesson on the works of this famous artist.

A Word on Words

This unit contains a great deal of mathematical vocabulary. We believe strongly that you should introduce and use mathematical words for communicating. Praise students for using correct terminology and finding words that precisely and accurately express their thoughts. Students learn words when they are given the opportunity to use them in discourse—it is unnecessary to require memorization. Words learned by rote are quickly forgotten. Encourage your students to use mathematical words in their group discussions both in and out of math class.

Several words require particular attention. When teaching children about regular figures, make sure they realize that the word **regular** has a special meaning in mathematics. A regular polygon is not an ordinary polygon, but rather a polygon with all sides and all angles equal. Another term that causes confusion is **right angle,** i.e., 90° angle. Researchers have found that it is not uncommon for children to believe that right angles open to the right, and left angles open to the left (Crowley, 1987). To avoid these errors, we have made many right angles open to the left as well as varying the orientation of angles in general.

Too often, geometry units in elementary textbooks focus on vocabulary and definitions. We hope the lessons in *Math Trailblazers* help students learn geometric words while actually exploring and discovering the fascinating world of geometry.

References

- Burger, W., and J.M. Shaughnessy. "Characterizing the van Hiele Levels of Development in Geometry." *Journal for Research in Mathematics Education,* 17, 31–48, National Council of Teachers of Mathematics, Reston, VA, 1986.

- Crowley, Mary L. "The van Hiele Model of the Development of Geometric Thought." *Learning and Teaching Geometry, K–12. 1987 Yearbook.* Edited by Mary Montgomery Lindquist. National Council of Teachers of Mathematics, Reston, VA, 1987.

- Fuys, D., D. Geddes, and R. Tischler. "The van Hiele Model of Thinking in Geometry Among Adolescents." *Journal for Research in Mathematics Education, Monograph Number 3.* National Council of Teachers of Mathematics, Reston, VA, 1988.

- Senk, Sharon L. "Van Hiele Levels and Achievement in Writing Geometry Proofs." *Journal for Research in Mathematics Education, vol 20, no. 3,* 309–321, National Council of Teachers of Mathematics, Reston, VA, 1989.

Observational Assessment Record

A1 Can students measure angles?

A2 Can students draw shapes and angles with given measures?

A3 Can students identify and describe 2-dimensional shapes?

A4 Can students classify 2-dimensional shapes?

A5 Can students identify congruent and similar shapes?

A6 Can students make and test conjectures about geometric properties?

A7 Can students use geometric concepts and skills to solve problems?

A8 Can students use numerical variables?

A9 Do students demonstrate fluency with the last six multiplication and division facts (4×6, 4×7, 4×8, 6×7, 6×8, 7×8)?

A10 _____

Name	A1	A2	A3	A4	A5	A6	A7	A8	A9	A10	Comments
1.											
2.											
3.											
4.											
5.											
6.											
7.											
8.											
9.											
10.											
11.											
12.											

Name	A1	A2	A3	A4	A5	A6	A7	A8	A9	A10	Comments
13.											
14.											
15.											
16.											
17.											
18.											
19.											
20.											
21.											
22.											
23.											
24.											
25.											
26.											
27.											
28.											
29.											
30.											
31.											
32.											

Unit 6

Daily Practice and Problems
Geometry

A DPP Menu for Unit 6

Two Daily Practice and Problems (DPP) items are included for each class session listed in the Unit Outline. A scope and sequence chart for the DPP is in the *Teacher Implementation Guide*.

Icons in the Teacher Notes column designate the subject matter of each DPP item. The first item in each class session is always a Bit and the second is either a Task or Challenge. Each item falls into one or more of the categories listed below. A menu of the DPP items for Unit 6 follows.

Ⓝ **Number Sense** A, H–K, O, P	✳ **Computation** D, H–J, N–P	⏱ **Time** K, N	⬙ **Geometry** C, F, L, M, R
⁵ₓ₇ **Math Facts** B, D, E, G, K, O–Q	$ **Money** N	⚖ **Measurement** C, F, L, M, R	◩ **Data** A

The *Daily Practice and Problems and Home Practice Guide* in the *Teacher Implementation Guide* includes information on how and when to use the DPP.

Review and Assessment of Math Facts

By the end of fourth grade, students in *Math Trailblazers* are expected to demonstrate fluency with all the multiplication and division facts. The DPP for this unit continues the systematic, strategies-based approach to reviewing the multiplication and division facts. This unit reviews the fifth and final group of facts, the last six facts— 4×6, 4×7, 4×8, 6×7, 6×8, and 7×8. These are called "the last six facts" because these facts are all that are left to learn after studying the 5s and 10s, 2s and 3s, squares, and 9s. The *Triangle Flash Cards* for these facts follow the Home Practice for this unit in the *Discovery*

Assignment Book. Blackline masters of all the cards, organized by group, are in the *Grade 5 Facts Resource Guide.*

The following describes how the facts will be practiced and assessed in the DPP for this unit.

1. DPP item B instructs students to quiz each other on the multiplication facts for the last six facts using the *Triangle Flash Cards.* Students sort the cards into three piles: those facts they know and can answer quickly, those they can figure out with a strategy, and those they need to learn. The DPP item also reminds students to update their *Multiplication* and *Division Facts I Know* charts, which they began in Lesson 2 of Unit 2.

2. DPP items D and E help students practice the multiplication facts for the last six facts. DPP item G uses fact families to review the related division facts.

3. DPP item Q assesses students on a mixture of multiplication and division facts. Students update both their *Multiplication* and *Division Facts I Know* charts.

Note: Part 1 of the Home Practice in the *Discovery Assignment Book* reminds students to take home their flash cards to practice the facts with a family member.

For more information about the distribution and assessment of the math facts, see the TIMS Tutor: *Math Facts* in the *Teacher Implementation Guide.* Also refer to the *Grade 5 Facts Resource Guide.*

Daily Practice and Problems

Students may solve the items individually, in groups, or as a class. The items may also be assigned for homework. The DPPs are also available on the Teacher Resource CD.

Student Questions	Teacher Notes

A Riding Bicycles

1. Jerome and John ride their bicycles at the same speed. It takes Jerome 15 minutes to ride 2 miles. How long does it take John to ride 5 miles?

2. Make a graph showing the distance Jerome and John travel and the time it takes. Put time on the horizontal axis and distance on the vertical axis. (*Hint:* Put a point on the graph to represent the time and distance when they start. What distance did they travel at 0 seconds?)

TIMS Bit

1. 37.5 minutes; Students might use equal ratios:

$$\frac{15\ minutes}{2\ miles} = \frac{37.5\ minutes}{5\ miles}$$

or $\frac{15\ minutes}{2\ miles} =$

$\frac{7.5\ minutes}{1\ mile}$,

$7.5 \times 5 = 37.5$ miles

2.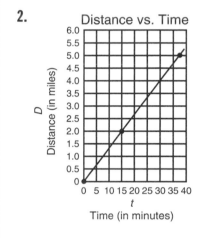

Multiplication and Division Facts: The Last Six Facts

With a partner, use your *Triangle Flash Cards* to quiz each other on the last six facts. Follow the directions in the *Student Guide* for Unit 2 Lesson 2.

As your partner quizzes you on the multiplication facts, separate the facts into three piles: those facts you know and can answer quickly, those you can figure out with a strategy, and those you need to learn. Practice the facts in the last two piles. List these facts so you can practice them at home. Repeat the process for the division facts.

Circle all the facts you know and can answer quickly on your *Multiplication* and *Division Facts I Know* charts.

TIMS Task

The *Triangle Flash Cards: Last Six Facts* follow the Home Practice in the *Discovery Assignment Book*. Blackline masters of all the flash cards, organized by group, are in the *Grade 5 Facts Resource Guide*. Part 1 of the Home Practice reminds students to take home the list of facts they need to study as well as their flash cards.

The *Multiplication* and *Division Facts I Know* charts were distributed in the *Unit Resource Guide* for Unit 2 Lesson 2. See the Lesson Guide or the *Grade 5 Facts Resource Guide* for more information.

Inform students when you will give the quiz on these facts. This quiz appears in DPP item Q.

Estimating Angles

Estimate the size of the angles your teacher creates for you.

TIMS Bit

Take two rulers and open them to form an angle. Students estimate the angle and give reasons to justify their answer. The teacher closes the rulers to zero and reopens them to form a new angle. In discussing strategies, encourage students to use the 90 degree or 180 degree angle for reference.

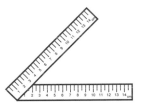

Variations:

1. Ask students to name the type of angle (acute, obtuse, right angle).

2. Say an angle measure or type of angle and ask students to use rulers or pencils to demonstrate the angle.

D **Choose Your Number Sentence**

Use each number once in any order with any operation sign (−, +, ×, ÷) to find the given answer. Remember, you can use parentheses, too.

6   3   15   2

A. _____ = 6

B. _____ = 14

C. _____ = 15

D. _____ = 7

E. Write a number sentence using each of these numbers once to get the smallest possible (whole number) answer.

F. Write a number sentence to give you the largest possible answer.

TIMS Challenge

One example is provided for each.

A. $(6 \times 3 - 15) \times 2 = 6$

B. $15 - 6 \div 2 \div 3 = 14$

C. $15 \times (6 - 3 - 2) = 15$

D. $6 \times 2 - 15 \div 3 = 7$

E. $15 - (6 \times 2 + 3) = 0$

F. $15 \times 6 \times 3 \times 2 = 540$

E **Practice with the Facts**

A. $4 \times 8 =$ B. $7 \times 6 =$

C. $6 \times 4 =$ D. $8 \times 6 =$

E. $4 \times 7 =$ F. $8 \times 7 =$

G. Describe a strategy for finding 8×7.

TIMS Bit

A. 32   B. 42

C. 24   D. 48

E. 28   F. 56

G. $8 \times 7 = 8 \times 5 + 8 \times 2 =$
   $40 + 16 = 56$

Strategies will vary.

F Measuring Area

A rectangular window is 4 feet high by $3\frac{1}{2}$ feet wide. Irma says the area is $12\frac{1}{2}$ square feet. Is she correct? If not, what is the area of the window? (*Hint:* Draw a picture on grid paper.)

TIMS Task

No. The correct area is 14 square feet.

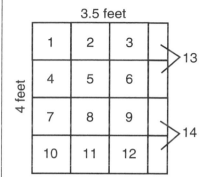

G Fact Families for × and ÷

Complete the number sentences for the related facts.

A. 4 × 7 = ___

___ ÷ 4 = ___

___ ÷ 7 = ___

___ × 4 = ___

B. 8 × 6 = ___

___ ÷ 8 = ___

___ ÷ 6 = ___

6 × ___ = ___

C. 6 × 7 = ___

___ ÷ 6 = ___

___ ÷ 7 = ___

___ × 6 = ___

D. 24 ÷ 6 = ___

___ × 6 = ___

24 ÷ ___ = ___

___ × 4 = ___

E. 8 × 7 = ___

___ ÷ 8 = ___

___ ÷ 7 = ___

___ × 8 = ___

F. 32 ÷ 8 = ___

4 × ___ = ___

___ ÷ 4 = ___

___ × 4 = ___

TIMS Bit

A. 28; 28 ÷ 4 = 7;
   28 ÷ 7 = 4;
   7 × 4 = 28

B. 48; 48 ÷ 8 = 6;
   48 ÷ 6 = 8;
   6 × 8 = 48

C. 42; 42 ÷ 6 = 7;
   42 ÷ 7 = 6;
   7 × 6 = 42

D. 4; 4 × 6 = 24;
   24 ÷ 4 = 6;
   6 × 4 = 24

E. 56; 56 ÷ 8 = 7;
   56 ÷ 7 = 8;
   7 × 8 = 56

F. 4; 4 × 8 = 32;
   32 ÷ 4 = 8;
   8 × 4 = 32

H Fractions

1. Choose the number closest to the actual sum:

    A. $\frac{7}{8} + \frac{12}{13}$ is closest to $\frac{1}{2}$, 1, $1\frac{1}{2}$, or 2?

    B. $\frac{4}{9} + \frac{5}{8}$ is closest to $\frac{1}{2}$, $\frac{3}{4}$, 1, or 2?

    C. $\frac{8}{9} - \frac{1}{12}$ is closest to 0, $\frac{1}{2}$, or 1?

    D. $\frac{1}{2} - \frac{4}{9}$ is closest to 0, $\frac{1}{4}$, or $\frac{1}{2}$?

2. Solve the following problems. Estimate using benchmarks such as $\frac{1}{2}$ to be sure your answers are reasonable. You may use any tools that you use in the classroom.

    A. $\frac{4}{5} + \frac{1}{2} =$ B. $\frac{7}{12} + \frac{1}{3} =$

    C. $\frac{5}{6} + \frac{3}{4} =$

TIMS Task

1. A. 2
   B. 1
   C. 1
   D. 0

2. A. $\frac{13}{10}$ or $1\frac{3}{10}$
   B. $\frac{11}{12}$
   C. $\frac{19}{12}$ or $1\frac{7}{12}$

I Practice

1. Estimate the answers to the following problems. Be ready to share your strategies with the class.

    A. $17 \times 56 =$ B. $1674 \div 4 =$

    C. $43 \times 77 =$

2. Solve the following problems using a paper-and-pencil method. Estimate to be sure your answers are reasonable.

    A. $870 \div 6 =$ B. $7045 \div 8 =$

    C. $34 \times 56 =$

TIMS Bit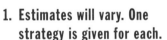

1. Estimates will vary. One strategy is given for each.
   A. $20 \times 50 = 1000$
   B. $1600 \div 4 = 400$;
        $74 \div 4$ is about 20;
        420 is a good estimate.
   C. $40 \times 80 = 3200$

2. A. 145
   B. 880 R5
   C. 1904

Sale!

The local department store is having a "10 percent off everything" sale.

A. About how much will a customer save on each item listed below?

B. Estimate the cost of each item on sale.

1. t-shirts are regularly $12.50 each

2. blue jeans are regularly $29.97 each

3. sweat shirts are regularly $22.50 each

4. jackets are regularly $67.40 each

5. sweaters are regularly $19.95 each

TIMS Challenge

Some possible answers:

1. A. $1.25
   B. $11.25; a little more than $11

2. A. about $3
   B. about $27

3. A. $2.25
   B. about $20

4. A. about $7
   B. about $60

5. A. about $2
   B. about $18

 Cristina's News Station

Cristina's News Station has 7 programs every half hour: the international news, local news, weather, traffic, advertising, Joke of the Day, and Today's Music Single. If each program is the same length, approximately how many minutes long is each program?

TIMS Bit

30 minutes ÷ 7 programs ≈ 4 minutes per program

Drawing Shapes

1. Draw triangle JKL using these directions:

    A. Make ∠K measure 70°.

    B. Make J̄K̄ measure 3 cm.

    C. Make K̄L̄ measure 5 cm.

1.

2. Draw triangle PQR using these directions:

    A. Make ∠Q measure 70°.

    B. Make P̄Q̄ twice the length of J̄K̄.

    C. Make Q̄R̄ twice the length of K̄L̄.

3. A. No, they are not the same size and shape.

    B. Yes, they are not the same size, but they are the same shape.

    C. Both angles have the same measurement, approximately 75°.

3. A. Are your two shapes congruent?

    B. Are they similar?

    C. Measure ∠J and ∠P. What do you find?

What's Your Angle?

Find the missing angle measurements.

1. A
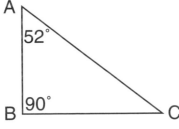
52°

B 90° C

2. ∠D, ∠E, and ∠F have the same measurement.

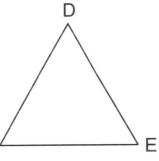

D

F   E

3. G 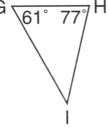 H
61° 77°

I

4. ∠J and ∠K have the same measurement.

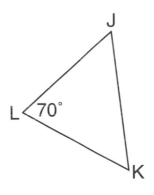

J

L 70°

K

TIMS Bit

1. 38°

2. Each angle is 60°.

3. 42°

4. Both angles are 55°.

Brandon the Babysitter

1. If Brandon earns $9 for 2 hours of babysitting, what is his hourly rate?

2. A. If Brandon needs $68.25 to buy a bike, how many hours will he need to babysit?

   B. Every school day this month Brandon walks his neighbor, a second grader, home from school. He babysits her from 3 to 5:30. How many days will it take Brandon to earn the money for the bike?

3. In the summer two families used Brandon as their babysitter. He worked 8 hours a week for each family. How much did he earn in one month? (Assume there are 4 weeks in 1 month.)

TIMS Task

1. $4.50 per hour

2. A. 16 hours

   B. 7 days; in 2 days he babysits 5 hours. After 6 days he will have babysat 15 hours. He will need 1 additional hour on the seventh day.

3. 8 hours × 2 = 16 hours a week; 16 hours × 4 weeks = 64 hours; 64 × $4.50 = $288.

 Multiplying and Dividing with Zeros

A. $80 \times 400 =$ B. $2800 \div 70 =$

C. $7 \times 80,000 =$ D. $700 \times 6000 =$

E. $4800 \div 600 =$ F. $240 \div 4 =$

TIMS Bit

A. 32,000   B. 40

C. 560,000   D. 4,200,000

E. 8   F. 60

P Number Sentences with 4, 6, 7, and 8

Use each number once in any order with any operation sign $(-, +, \times, \div)$ to write number sentences. You can also use parentheses. Use these numbers: 4, 6, 7, 8.

(Remember, you must use each number once, but only once.)

A. _____ = 1

B. _____ = 10

C. _____ = 20

D. _____ = 200

TIMS Challenge

One example is provided for each.

A. $8 \div 4 - (7 - 6) = 1$

B. $4 \times 6 \div 8 + 7 = 10$

C. $8 \times 6 - 7 \times 4 = 20$

D. $(7 \times 8 - 6) \times 4 = 200$

Q Quiz: The Last Six Facts

A. $6 \times 7 =$ B. $24 \div 6 =$

C. $8 \times 7 =$ D. $7 \times 4 =$

E. $48 \div 8 =$ F. $32 \div 4 =$

TIMS Bit

We recommend 1 minute for this quiz. Allow students to change pens after the time is up and complete the remaining problems in a different color. After students take the test, have them update their *Multiplication Facts I Know* and *Division Facts I Know* charts.

Is It Possible?

You may need to experiment to find these answers. Explain your answers in words or pictures.

1. Can a triangle have two right angles?

2. If two angles of a triangle are equal, does the third angle also have to be equal to the other two angles?

3. If a triangle has two equal sides, can its angles all be different sizes?

TIMS Challenge

Your students may notice that one counterexample is enough to prove something false. Proving something true is harder, but a good demonstration shows understanding.

1. No. Two right angles prevent the drawing of a triangle. The shape would have to be at least 4-sided.

2. No. It does not have to be equal. The third angle could be different, in which case the third side will be different, forming an isosceles triangle.

3. No. Students should construct triangles with two equal sides and then determine if the angles are different.

Lesson 1

Angle Measures

Lesson Overview

Estimated Class Sessions

2

Students review angles and estimate angle measures using benchmarks (90°, 180°, and 270° angles). Measuring with a protractor is also reviewed. Students then practice drawing angles.

Key Content

- Estimating angle measures using benchmarks.
- Measuring angles with a protractor.
- Drawing angles of determined degrees.
- Identifying acute, obtuse, and right angles.

Key Vocabulary

- acute angle
- angle
- degree (°)
- endpoint
- obtuse angle
- protractor
- ray
- right angle
- sides
- straight angle
- vertex

Math Facts

Complete DPP items B and D for this lesson. Task B begins the review of the last six facts, while Challenge D uses operations to solve puzzles.

Homework

1. Students complete homework *Questions 1–5* in the *Student Guide* after Part 1.
2. Students complete homework *Questions 6–8* in the *Student Guide* after Part 2.
3. Assign Part 1 of the Home Practice. Students use flash cards to review the last six facts.

Assessment

1. Use *Question 8* in the Homework section in the *Student Guide* as an assessment.
2. Use the *Observational Assessment Record* to note students' abilities to measure angles.

Curriculum Sequence

Before This Unit

Students were introduced to angles in Unit 2 of fourth grade. They measured angles and drew angles in Unit 9 of fourth grade. The terms line, line segment, and ray were discussed in Unit 9 Lesson 1 of fourth grade.

After This Unit

Angles will be explored further in Unit 10.

Materials List

Supplies and Copies

Student	Teacher
Supplies for Each Student • protractor • cardboard corners, optional	**Supplies** • protractor • cardboard corners, optional
Copies	**Copies/Transparencies** • 1 transparency of *Measuring Angles,* optional (*Discovery Assignment Book* Pages 87–88) • 1 copy of *Observational Assessment Record* to be used throughout this unit (*Unit Resource Guide* Pages 11–12)

All blackline masters including assessment, transparency, and DPP masters are also on the Teacher Resource CD.

Student Books

Angle Measures (*Student Guide* Pages 184–191)
Triangle Flash Cards: Last Six Facts (*Discovery Assignment Book* Pages 85–86)
Measuring Angles (*Discovery Assignment Book* Pages 87–88)

Daily Practice and Problems and Home Practice

DPP items A–D (*Unit Resource Guide* Pages 15–18)
Home Practice Part 1 (*Discovery Assignment Book* Page 81)

Note: Classrooms whose pacing differs significantly from the suggested pacing of the units should use the Math Facts Calendar in Section 4 of the *Facts Resource Guide* to ensure students receive the complete math facts program.

Assessment Tools

Observational Assessment Record (*Unit Resource Guide* Pages 11–12)

Daily Practice and Problems

Suggestions for using the DPPs are on page 36.

A. Bit: Riding Bicycles (URG p. 15)

1. Jerome and John ride their bicycles at the same speed. It takes Jerome 15 minutes to ride 2 miles. How long does it take John to ride 5 miles?

2. Make a graph showing the distance Jerome and John travel and the time it takes. Put time on the horizontal axis and distance on the vertical axis. (*Hint:* Put a point on the graph to represent the time and distance when they start. What distance did they travel at 0 seconds?)

B. Task: Multiplication and Division Facts: The Last Six Facts (URG p. 16)

With a partner, use your *Triangle Flash Cards* to quiz each other on the last six facts. Follow the directions in the *Student Guide* for Unit 2 Lesson 2.

As your partner quizzes you on the multiplication facts, separate the facts into three piles: those facts you know and can answer quickly, those you can figure out with a strategy, and those you need to learn. Practice the facts in the last two piles. List these facts so you can practice them at home. Repeat the process for the division facts.

Circle all the facts you know and can answer quickly on your *Multiplication* and *Division Facts I Know* charts.

C. Bit: Estimating Angles (URG p. 17)

Estimate the size of the angles your teacher creates for you.

D. Challenge: Choose Your Number Sentence (URG p. 18)

Use each number once in any order with any operation sign (−, +, ×, ÷) to find the given answer. Remember, you can use parentheses, too.

6   3   15   2

A. _____ = 6

B. _____ = 14

C. _____ = 15

D. _____ = 7

E. Write a number sentence using each of these numbers once to get the smallest possible (whole number) answer.

F. Write a number sentence to give you the largest possible answer.

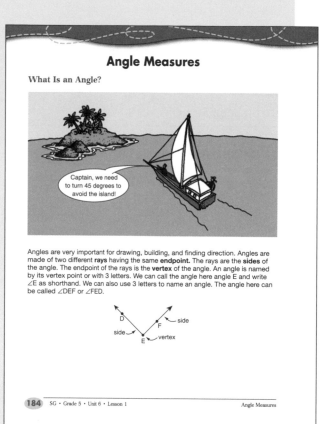

Angle Measures

What Is an Angle?

Angles are very important for drawing, building, and finding direction. Angles are made of two different **rays** having the same **endpoint**. The rays are the **sides** of the angle. The endpoint of the rays is the **vertex** of the angle. An angle is named by its vertex point or with 3 letters. We can call the angle here angle E and write ∠E as shorthand. We can also use 3 letters to name an angle. The angle here can be called ∠DEF or ∠FED.

Student Guide - page 184

Content Note

Angles. The **sides of an angle** are two rays with the same **endpoint.** A **ray** is part of a line with one endpoint. The endpoint is called the **vertex** of the angle. The number of degrees measures the amount of turning of an angle. Another way to say this is that the **degrees** describe the amount of opening of an angle.

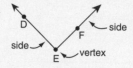

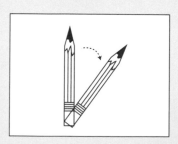

Figure 1: *Forming an angle*

Figure 2: *Making angles with scissors*

Before the Activity

Some teachers find it helpful to cut right triangles from cardboard so students have a tool for checking whether an angle is acute, obtuse, or right. These triangles can then be used year after year.

Teaching the Activity

In the first part of this lesson, students review the notion that an **angle** is an amount of turning or the amount of opening between two rays. The second part provides practice in using a protractor. If students understand what an angle is and how to measure and draw angles, you may move through the lesson quickly, reviewing only as needed. This lesson contains many vocabulary words. Students will learn these words through discourse. There is no need to require memorization.

Part 1 **What Is an Angle?**

Ask students to stand with one hand outstretched in front of them and slowly turn completely around. Ask them what they just did mathematically. Compare their hand to a hand of a clock as it makes a rotation. Someone should say they turned 360 degrees.

Remind students that turning a complete circle is turning 360 degrees (this is by definition). Write 360° on the board and explain that the ° symbol is a shorthand way of writing degrees. Ask:

If turning a whole circle is 360°, then:
- *How many degrees do you turn when you turn a half circle?* (180°)
- *How many degrees do you turn when you turn a quarter circle?* (90°)
- *How many degrees do you turn when you turn three-quarters of a circle?* (270°)

Do several more of these. You may have students turn 90° to the left, 270° to the right, and so on.

Explain to students that we talk about the angles formed by turns. Students made angles as they turned. As another example, hold two pencils or rulers together. Slowly move one of the pencils (or rulers) to show the formation of an angle as illustrated in Figure 1. Make several angles like this and have students guess about how many degrees you turned. Suggest students use 90°, 180°, and 270° as benchmarks. The pencils represent the sides of the angle.

To reinforce the idea that the amount of turning (or the opening) of the angle and not the length of sides determines the angle, use two pairs of scissors that are different in size as Figure 2 illustrates.

Do several demonstrations, each time asking students which angle is bigger:

- Open the larger pair of scissors wider to make an angle bigger than the angle formed by the smaller pair.
- Open the smaller pair wider to make an angle bigger than the angle formed by the larger pair.
- Open both pairs the same amount.

Use other objects in the classroom to illustrate that the size of the angle does not depend on the lengths of the sides, but on the amount of opening. For example, have a student make an angle using 2 metersticks while another student makes an angle using 2 rulers. Have the class estimate the size of the angles.

When students seem comfortable forming angles by an action, explain that many angles already exist around us. The hands of the clock form angles. Ask students to look around the room and find more examples of angles. The corners of the classroom are another example of 90°. In fact, the two walls and floor make three right angles. Students may note corners of books, papers, or boxes. Discuss the sides and vertices of the angles. Ask students to find angles that do not appear to be 90°.

Draw several angles on the board or overhead and ask students to estimate their measures. Encourage them to use 90°, 180°, and 270° as benchmarks. Ask:

- *Does this angle appear to be greater than 90°? How much greater? More than halfway between 90° and 180°?*

Draw some angles opening to the left, or opening down. Draw some angles with short sides and some with uneven sides as in Figure 3. This helps children realize that it is the amount of opening that is important, not the sides.

Remind students that the vertex of an angle is a point and is often named with a letter. By convention, we refer to an angle by the name of the vertex, if it causes no confusion. Otherwise, we use three letters to name an angle. For example, we can refer to ∠A or ∠CAB or ∠BAC in Figure 4, where B and C are points on the sides of the angle. Note that the vertex is the middle letter in the three-letter name.

Remind students that an angle that measures 90° is called a **right angle.** Angles that measure less than 90° are **acute angles** and angles that measure more than 90° but less than 180° are **obtuse angles.** A **straight angle** is an angle that measures 180°.

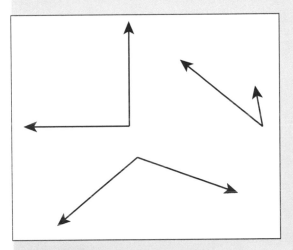

Student Guide - page 185

Figure 3: *Various angles*

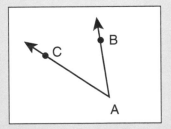

Figure 4: *Naming angles*

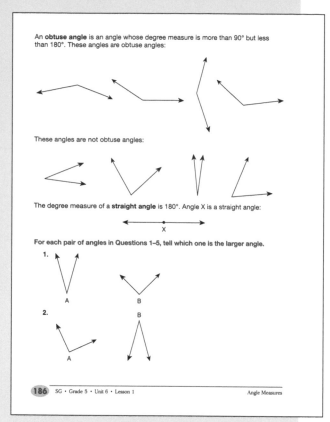

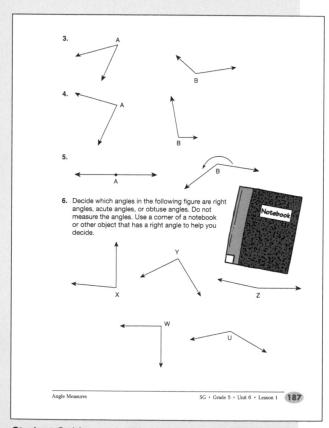

We frequently need to draw or measure 90° angles. To do this, a cardboard corner or other object that has a 90° angle can be used. Draw angles that are close to 90° on the overhead or board. (A freehand sketch is fine.) Ask students to estimate whether or not the various angles are 90°. Ask students to come to the board or overhead and determine whether the angle you drew was indeed less than 90, greater than 90, or 90 degrees (i.e., acute, obtuse, or right) using a corner as shown in Figure 5. If the other side of the angle is covered by the paper, the angle is less than 90°. If the other side of the angle "sticks out," the angle is larger than 90°.

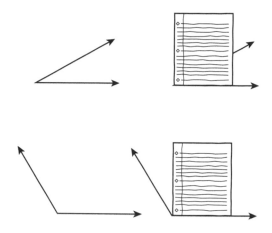

Figure 5: *Using a square corner*

Ask students to read and discuss the What Is an Angle? section on the *Angle Measures* Activity Pages in the *Student Guide.* Be sure to point out the angles in **Question 5.** Whenever we draw an angle, we actually draw two angles. Unless otherwise noted, we are referring to the smaller angle. However, to make clear in **Question 5** that we are interested in the larger angle, we draw an arrow. This is illustrated in Figure 6.

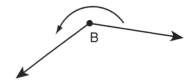

Figure 6: *The angle referenced here is the larger of the 2 angles.*

In **Question 6,** encourage students to use a cardboard corner, sheet of paper, book, or other object to decide whether the angles are right, obtuse, or acute.

You can assign Homework **Questions 1–5** after Part 1.

Part 2 Using a Protractor

Explain to students that we can use a **protractor** to measure angles. Remind students that you are measuring the amount of or turning between the two sides of the angle. Use a clear protractor or transparency of a protractor directly on an overhead projector for discussion.

Point out that there are usually two sets of numbers from 0 to 180 on the protractor—one appearing clockwise, the other counterclockwise. Remind students that a 180° turn is half a circle, while a 360° turn is a full circle. Explain that one of the sides (or rays) of the angle to be measured must always be on the bottom line (the 0 degree line) and the vertex of the angle must be in the center of this line segment. Some protractors have a hole at the center. Make sure students understand to use the set of numbers that begins where one of the sides of the angle lies. For example, since a side of the angle in Figure 7 lies on the left side of the hole, we use the outer set of numbers to read the angle measure correctly as 46°. Remind students to look at the angle and determine by sight whether the angle is greater than or less than 90°. This will reduce the number of errors.

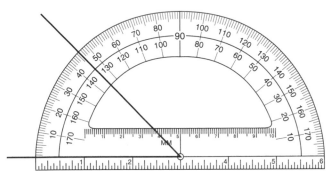

Figure 7: *Angle measuring 46°*

If the measure of angle A is 46 degrees, we use a shorthand notation and write ∠A = 46°.

TIMS Tip

Some protractors begin the numbering scale at the very bottom edge of the protractor. That is, the 0 degree line is the bottom edge of the protractor. If any of your students have such protractors, make sure they are able to use them correctly.

Content Note

Strictly speaking, there is a difference between an angle and its measure. However, as the meaning is clear here, we use the shorthand notation and write ∠A = 46° to mean the measure of ∠A is 46°.

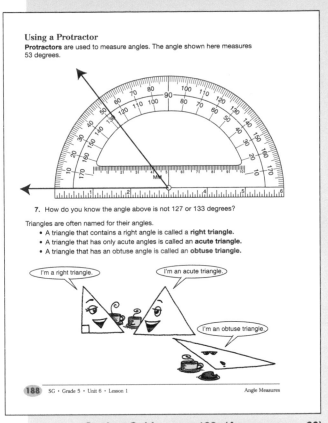

Using a Protractor
Protractors are used to measure angles. The angle shown here measures 53 degrees.

7. How do you know the angle above is not 127 or 133 degrees?

Triangles are often named for their angles.
- A triangle that contains a right angle is called a **right triangle.**
- A triangle that has only acute angles is called an **acute triangle.**
- A triangle that has an obtuse angle is called an **obtuse triangle.**

I'm a right triangle. I'm an acute triangle.

I'm an obtuse triangle.

188   SG • Grade 5 • Unit 6 • Lesson 1   Angle Measures

Student Guide - page 188 (Answers on p. 39)

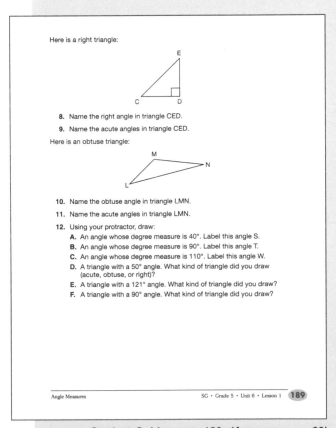

Here is a right triangle:

8. Name the right angle in triangle CED.
9. Name the acute angles in triangle CED.

Here is an obtuse triangle:

10. Name the obtuse angle in triangle LMN.
11. Name the acute angles in triangle LMN.
12. Using your protractor, draw:
    A. An angle whose degree measure is 40°. Label this angle S.
    B. An angle whose degree measure is 90°. Label this angle T.
    C. An angle whose degree measure is 110°. Label this angle W.
    D. A triangle with a 50° angle. What kind of triangle did you draw (acute, obtuse, or right)?
    E. A triangle with a 121° angle. What kind of triangle did you draw?
    F. A triangle with a 90° angle. What kind of triangle did you draw?

Angle Measures   SG • Grade 5 • Unit 6 • Lesson 1   **189**

Student Guide - page 189 (Answers on p. 39)

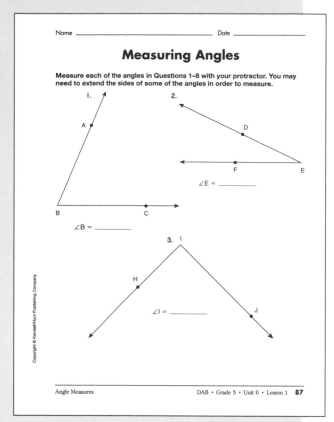

Name _____ Date _____

Measuring Angles

Measure each of the angles in Questions 1–8 with your protractor. You may need to extend the sides of some of the angles in order to measure.

1.

∠B = _____

2.

∠E = _____

3.

∠I = _____

Discovery Assignment Book - page 87 (Answers on p. 41)

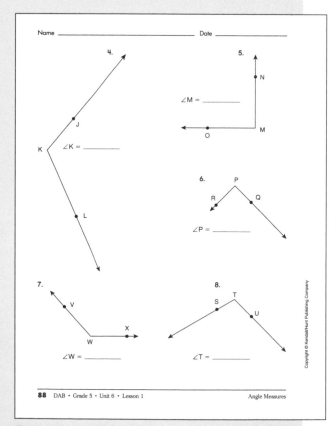

Name _____ Date _____

4.

∠K = _____

5.

∠M = _____

6.

∠P = _____

7.

∠W = _____

8.

∠T = _____

Discovery Assignment Book - page 88 (Answers on p. 41)

Have students practice measuring angles using the *Measuring Angles* Activity Pages in the *Discovery Assignment Book.* Have students complete ***Questions 1–4.*** Use transparencies of these pages to discuss the angles together. Have students refer to the angles by different names. For example, ∠ABC can also be called ∠CBA or just ∠B.

Content Note

Accuracy of Measurement. It is important for children to understand the limits of accuracy in measuring. While we measure an angle and say it is 90°, the accuracy is at best to the nearest degree. Note that the measurement tools we have available are not very precise. Engineers, architects, and other professionals have tools that are much more accurate, but no tool is perfect. In work with angle measures, accept measures that are off by a degree or two because of the imprecision of measurement tools, line thickness, and other factors.

Before students complete ***Questions 5–8*** on the *Measuring Angles* Activity Pages in the *Discovery Assignment Book,* draw on the overhead or board an angle whose sides are not long enough to reach the scale on the protractor. Ask:

• *What should you do to measure this angle accurately?* (Students will suggest extending the sides of the angle to measure accurately.)

Explain to students that it is often necessary to extend an angle's sides when measuring figures containing several angles. Remind them that the sides of an angle are rays. Rays by definition go on forever in one direction so they may extend the sides with a straightedge as long as they like. Students should finish measuring the angles in ***Questions 5–8*** on the *Measuring Angles* Activity Pages. The sides of these angles need to be extended.

To practice recognizing angles and naming them, draw a figure similar to Figure 8 on the board or overhead projector. Ask:

• *Name the three angles in the figure.* (∠DEF, ∠DEG, ∠FEG)

• *Explain why it is not a good idea to refer to ∠E.* (It is not clear which angle is being referenced.)

Measure these angles together as a class and decide which are obtuse, acute, or right angles. Students should see that the sum of the measures of the smaller two angles equals the measure of the larger angle.

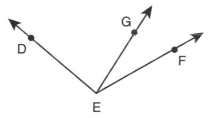

Figure 8: *Three angles*

Students may need help recognizing angles in shapes. Draw several polygons like the ones shown in Figure 9 on the overhead or board. Ask students to count first the number of angles in the interior of each shape and then to name the angles. For example, the first shape shown in Figure 9 has 4 angles. The four angles could be named ∠X, ∠Y, ∠Z, and ∠W. Another way to name these angles is ∠YXW, ∠XWZ, ∠WZY, and ∠ZYX. Then, ask them to estimate the measures of the angles using a right corner.

Content Note

Interior Angles of Polygons. Whenever we refer to the angles of a polygon, we are referring to the interior angles of the polygon.

Review drawing angles of specific degrees by asking the class to draw an angle of, say, 50°. Illustrate, as shown in Figure 10, how to draw an angle. First, students should use the edge of their protractor or a ruler to make one side of the angle and pick a point for the vertex. Then, they should place the protractor so the vertex is on the hole in the protractor and the drawn side of the angle matches the 0° line. Mark with a point the desired degrees as shown in Figure 10. Then use the straightedge to draw the line between the dot and the vertex.

The Using a Protractor section of the *Angle Measures* Activity Pages in the *Student Guide* reviews the material discussed in class. It also reviews the definitions for right, obtuse, and acute triangles. Have students complete ***Questions 7–12.*** You can assign Homework ***Questions 6–8.***

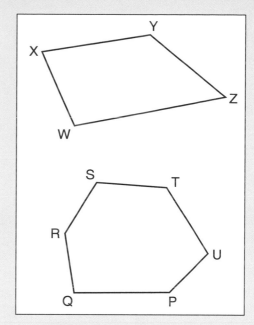

Figure 9: *Angles in shapes*

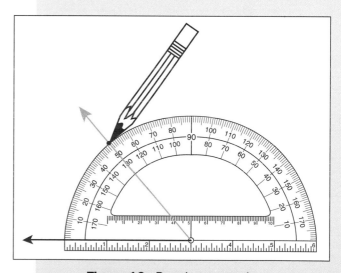

Figure 10: *Drawing an angle*

Math Facts

DPP item B begins the review of the multiplication and division facts for the last six facts.

Homework and Practice

- Assign DPP item A, which reviews making and interpreting line graphs.

- Students can complete Homework **Questions 1–5** on the *Angle Measures* Activity Pages in the *Student Guide* after Part 1 of the lesson.

- You can assign Homework **Questions 6–8** for homework after Part 2.

- Use DPP Bit C to practice naming acute, obtuse, and right angles.

- Assign Part 1 of the Home Practice, which reviews the last six facts.

Assessment

- Use homework **Question 8** to assess students' abilities to draw angles.

- Use the *Observational Assessment Record* to note students' abilities to measure angles.

Extension

Challenge D uses addition, subtraction, multiplication, and division to solve number sentence puzzles.

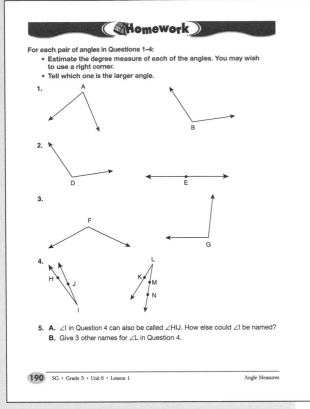

Student Guide - page 190 *(Answers on p. 40)*

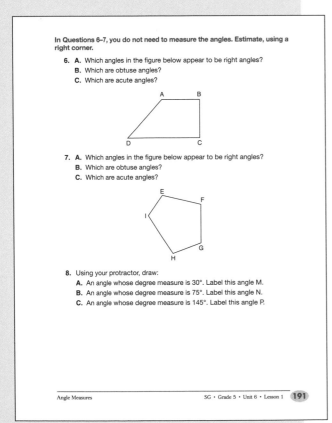

Student Guide - page 191 *(Answers on p. 40)*

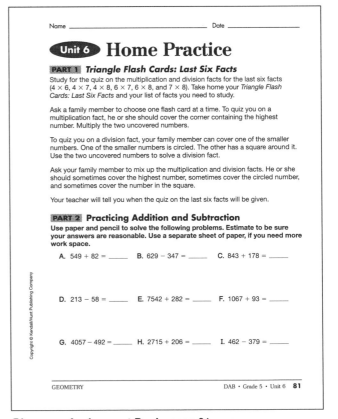

Discovery Assignment Book - page 81

At a Glance

Math Facts and Daily Practice and Problems

Complete DPP items A–D for this lesson. Task B begins the review of the last six facts, while Challenge D uses operations to solve puzzles.

Part 1. What Is an Angle?

1. Students demonstrate moving 360, 270, 180, and 90 degrees.
2. Discuss the parts of an angle (vertex and sides).
3. Illustrate and discuss that the size of the opening (or the amount of turning) determines the angle, not the length of the sides.
4. Discuss how to name angles with letters.
5. Discuss acute, obtuse, and right angles.
6. Practice estimating angle measures using benchmarks (90°, 180°, 270°).
7. Students complete the What Is an Angle? section of the *Angle Measures* Activity Pages in the *Student Guide. (Questions 1–6)*

Part 2. Using a Protractor

1. Discuss how to use a protractor to measure angles.
2. Students complete the *Measuring Angles* Activity Pages in the *Discovery Assignment Book.*
3. Discuss naming angles in shapes.
4. Draw shapes on the board and ask students to identify angles, name them, and estimate their measure.
5. Discuss how to draw angles of determined degree measure using a protractor.
6. Students complete the Using a Protractor section of the *Angle Measures* Activity Pages in the *Student Guide. (Questions 7–12)*

Homework

1. Students complete homework *Questions 1–5* in the *Student Guide* after Part 1.
2. Students complete homework *Questions 6–8* in the *Student Guide* after Part 2.
3. Assign Part 1 of the Home Practice. Students use flash cards to review the last six facts.

Assessment

1. Use *Question 8* in the Homework section in the *Student Guide* as an assessment.
2. Use the *Observational Assessment Record* to note students' abilities to measure angles.

Extension

Assign DPP Challenge D.

Answer Key is on pages 38–41.

Notes:

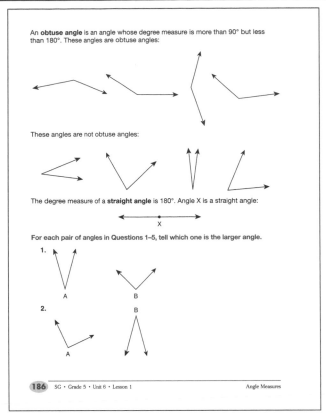

Student Guide - page 186

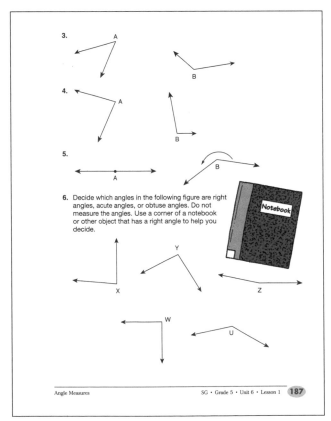

Student Guide - page 187

Student Guide (pp. 186–187)

1. ∠B

2. ∠A

3. ∠B

4. ∠B

5. ∠B

6. right: W; acute: X; obtuse: U, Y, and Z

Student Guide (pp. 188–189)

7. You can tell it is an acute angle so it must be less than 90 degrees.

8. ∠D

9. ∠C and ∠E

10. ∠M

11. ∠L and ∠N

12. A.

40°
S

B.

90°
T

C.

110°
W

D. Answers will vary.

E. Answers will vary; an obtuse triangle.

F. Answers will vary; a right triangle.

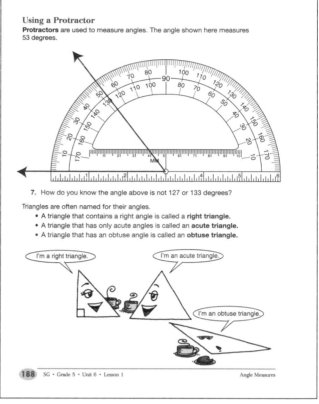

Student Guide - page 188

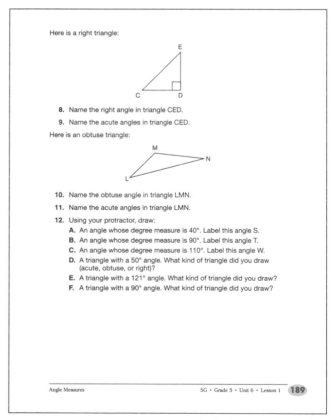

Student Guide - page 189

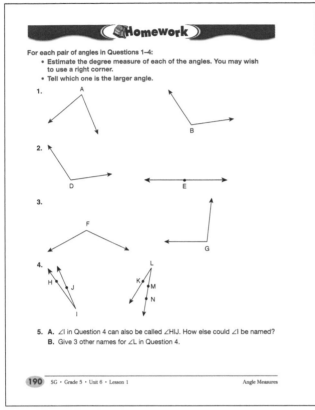

Student Guide - page 190

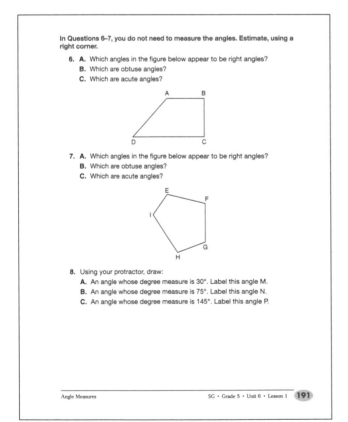

Student Guide - page 191

Student Guide (pp. 190–191)

Homework

Estimates will vary.

1. ∠B

2. ∠E

3. ∠F

4. ∠L

5. **A.** ∠JIH

   B. ∠KLM, ∠MLK, ∠NLK, and ∠KLN

6. **A.** ∠B and ∠C

   B. ∠A

   C. ∠D

7. **A.** none

   B. ∠E, ∠F, ∠G, ∠H, and ∠I

   C. none

8. **A.**

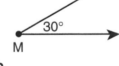

   B.

   C.

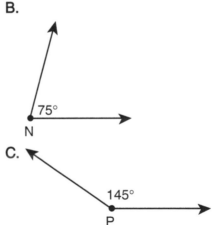

Discovery Assignment Book (pp. 87–88)

Measuring Angles

1. 68°
2. 26°
3. 90°
4. 116°
5. 90°
6. 90°
7. 132°
8. 105°

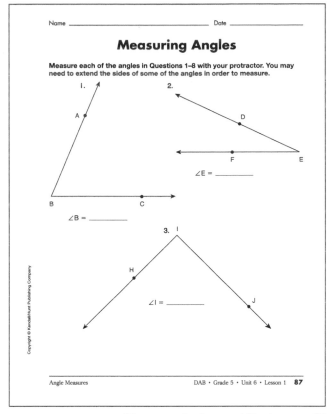

Discovery Assignment Book - page 87

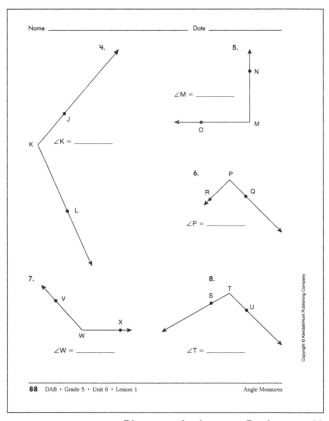

Discovery Assignment Book - page 88

Lesson 2

Angles in Triangles and Other Polygons

Estimated Class Sessions

2

Lesson Overview

Students measure angles in polygons. Polygons, including regular polygons, are discussed. Students discover that the sum of the interior angles of a triangle is always 180 degrees.

Key Content

- Measuring angles.
- Investigating properties of regular polygons.
- Demonstrating that the sum of the angles in a triangle is 180°.
- Identifying acute, obtuse, and right angles.

Key Vocabulary

- polygon
- quadrilateral
- regular polygon
- trapezoid

Math Facts

Complete DPP items E and G for this lesson. Item E provides practice with the last six facts. Item G introduces fact families.

Homework

1. Assign *Questions 1–6* in the Homework section of the *Student Guide* after Part 1.
2. Assign *Questions 7–9* in the Homework section after Part 2.
3. Assign Parts 2 and 3 of the Home Practice.

Assessment

1. Use DPP item M as an assessment.
2. Use the *Observational Assessment Record* to document students' abilities to identify, describe, and classify 2D shapes.

Materials List

Supplies and Copies

Student	Teacher
Supplies for Each Student • protractor • ruler • scissors • 2 blank unlined sheets of paper • cardboard corners, optional **Supplies for Each Student Group** • 1 set of pattern blocks (6 green triangles and at least 1 of each of the following: yellow hexagon, red trapezoid, blue rhombus, brown trapezoid, purple triangle, tan rhombus, and orange square) • pattern block templates, optional	**Supplies** • protractor • ruler • cardboard corners or plastic right triangle • pattern block templates, optional • overhead pattern blocks, optional • large blackboard protractor, optional
TIMS Tip To organize the pattern blocks for this geometry activity, add tan rhombuses and orange squares to the sets of pattern blocks used in the fraction activities in Units 3 and 5.	**Copies/Transparencies** • 1 transparency of *Measuring Pattern Block Angles*, optional (*Discovery Assignment Book* Pages 89–90) • 1 transparency of *Regular Polygons* (*Unit Resource Guide* Page 52)

All blackline masters including assessment, transparency, and DPP masters are also on the Teacher Resource CD.

Student Books
Angles in Triangles and Other Polygons (*Student Guide* Pages 192–196)
Measuring Pattern Block Angles (*Discovery Assignment Book* Pages 89–90)

Daily Practice and Problems and Home Practice
DPP items E–H (*Unit Resource Guide* Pages 18–20)
Home Practice Parts 2–3 (*Discovery Assignment Book* Pages 81–82)

Note: Classrooms whose pacing differs significantly from the suggested pacing of the units should use the Math Facts Calendar in Section 4 of the *Facts Resource Guide* to ensure students receive the complete math facts program.

Assessment Tools
Observational Assessment Record (*Unit Resource Guide* Pages 11–12)

E. Bit: Practice with the Facts (URG p. 18)

A. $4 \times 8 =$ B. $7 \times 6 =$
C. $6 \times 4 =$ D. $8 \times 6 =$
E. $4 \times 7 =$ F. $8 \times 7 =$
G. Describe a strategy for finding 8×7.

F. Task: Measuring Area (URG p. 19)

A rectangular window is 4 feet high by $3\frac{1}{2}$ feet wide. Irma says the area is $12\frac{1}{2}$ square feet. Is she correct? If not, what is the area of the window? (*Hint:* Draw a picture on grid paper.)

G. Bit: Fact Families for $\times$ and $\div$
    (URG p. 19)

Complete the number sentences for the related facts.

A. $4 \times 7 = \underline{\hspace{0.4cm}}$ B. $8 \times 6 = \underline{\hspace{0.4cm}}$

$\underline{\hspace{0.4cm}} \div 4 = \underline{\hspace{0.4cm}}$ $\underline{\hspace{0.4cm}} \div 8 = \underline{\hspace{0.4cm}}$

$\underline{\hspace{0.4cm}} \div 7 = \underline{\hspace{0.4cm}}$ $\underline{\hspace{0.4cm}} \div 6 = \underline{\hspace{0.4cm}}$

$\underline{\hspace{0.4cm}} \times 4 = \underline{\hspace{0.4cm}}$ $6 \times \underline{\hspace{0.4cm}} = \underline{\hspace{0.4cm}}$

C. $6 \times 7 = \underline{\hspace{0.4cm}}$ D. $24 \div 6 = \underline{\hspace{0.4cm}}$

$\underline{\hspace{0.4cm}} \div 6 = \underline{\hspace{0.4cm}}$ $\underline{\hspace{0.4cm}} \times 6 = \underline{\hspace{0.4cm}}$

$\underline{\hspace{0.4cm}} \div 7 = \underline{\hspace{0.4cm}}$ $24 \div \underline{\hspace{0.4cm}} = \underline{\hspace{0.4cm}}$

$\underline{\hspace{0.4cm}} \times 6 = \underline{\hspace{0.4cm}}$ $\underline{\hspace{0.4cm}} \times 4 = \underline{\hspace{0.4cm}}$

E. $8 \times 7 = \underline{\hspace{0.4cm}}$ F. $32 \div 8 = \underline{\hspace{0.4cm}}$

$\underline{\hspace{0.4cm}} \div 8 = \underline{\hspace{0.4cm}}$ $4 \times \underline{\hspace{0.4cm}} = \underline{\hspace{0.4cm}}$

$\underline{\hspace{0.4cm}} \div 7 = \underline{\hspace{0.4cm}}$ $\underline{\hspace{0.4cm}} \div 4 = \underline{\hspace{0.4cm}}$

$\underline{\hspace{0.4cm}} \times 8 = \underline{\hspace{0.4cm}}$ $\underline{\hspace{0.4cm}} \times 4 = \underline{\hspace{0.4cm}}$

H. Task: Fractions (URG p. 20)

1. Choose the number closest to the actual sum:

    A. $\frac{7}{8} + \frac{12}{13}$ is closest to $\frac{1}{2}$, 1, $1\frac{1}{2}$, or 2?

    B. $\frac{4}{9} + \frac{5}{8}$ is closest to $\frac{1}{2}$, $\frac{3}{4}$, 1, or 2?

    C. $\frac{8}{9} - \frac{1}{12}$ is closest to 0, $\frac{1}{2}$, or 1?

    D. $\frac{1}{2} - \frac{4}{9}$ is closest to 0, $\frac{1}{4}$, or $\frac{1}{2}$?

2. Solve the following problems. Estimate using benchmarks such as $\frac{1}{2}$ to be sure your answers are reasonable. You may use any tools that you use in the classroom.

    A. $\frac{4}{5} + \frac{1}{2} =$ B. $\frac{7}{12} + \frac{1}{3} =$

    C. $\frac{5}{6} + \frac{3}{4} =$

If students measured the angles of the pattern blocks in fourth grade (Unit 2 Lesson 7), you can move quickly through the beginning of this lesson.

Part 1 **Angles in Polygons**

Draw a quadrilateral on the overhead or board and label the vertices A, B, C, and D. Ask volunteers to come up to measure the angles. If any of the angles have sides that are not long enough to reach the scale of the protractor, show students that they can extend the sides of a quadrilateral as in Figure 11.

To practice measuring angles in shapes, draw several more polygons for student pairs to measure on the overhead or board. As one student measures, the other closely watches to see that he or she is accurate. Be sure to include angles small enough that students have to extend the sides of some of them.

Explain to students that the figures you draw are called polygons. The word *polygon* means many (*poly*) angled (*gon*). A **polygon** is a many-sided (or angled) figure. Point out to students that a polygon is made up of line segments that are all connected. The sides of a polygon never overlap, and a polygon is a closed figure. That is, each endpoint of every side meets with the endpoint of one other side. Figure 12 provides some examples of figures that are and are not polygons.

Explain that the figure in Figure 11 is a quadrilateral. A **quadrilateral** is a polygon with four sides. The prefix *quad* means four and the suffix *lateral* means sides. To communicate easily about figures, we often give the vertices names (usually letters, just as we do with angles) and call the quadrilateral by the names of the vertices, going in clockwise or counterclockwise order.

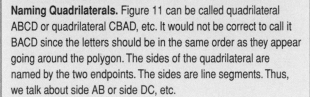

Content Note

Naming Quadrilaterals. Figure 11 can be called quadrilateral ABCD or quadrilateral CBAD, etc. It would not be correct to call it BACD since the letters should be in the same order as they appear going around the polygon. The sides of the quadrilateral are named by the two endpoints. The sides are line segments. Thus, we talk about side AB or side DC, etc.

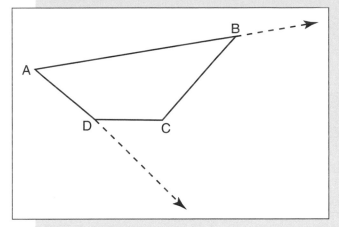

Figure 11: *Measuring the angles of a quadrilateral*

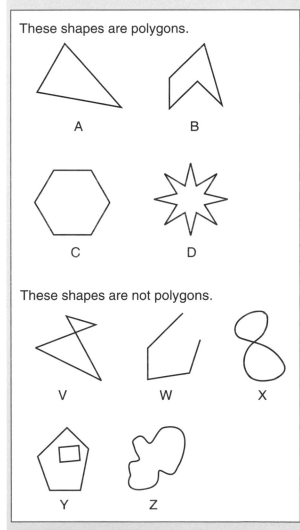

These shapes are polygons.

A   B

C   D

These shapes are not polygons.

V   W   X

Y   Z

Figure 12: *Polygons and shapes that are not polygons*

Trace a red pattern block trapezoid on the overhead projector (or draw the trapezoid using a pattern block template). Be sure to make the angles sharp so they are easy to measure. See Figure 13. Label the vertices so it is easier to talk about the four angles. From Unit 3, students should know this shape to be a trapezoid. Note that the trapezoid is also a quadrilateral (and a polygon). We will define a **trapezoid** as a quadrilateral with exactly one pair of parallel sides. Remind students that **parallel lines** are lines that do not intersect or cross. Ask for volunteers to measure the angles. Since the sides of the trapezoid are not long enough to reach the scale on the protractor, students will need to extend the sides.

Figure 13: *The red trapezoid*

Students should complete the *Measuring Pattern Block Angles* Activity Pages in the *Discovery Assignment Book.* Encourage students to use shortcuts to find the angle measures of the pattern blocks. Students can figure out many angle measures by placing the green triangle on top of the shape. For example, two green triangles make the blue rhombus. See Figure 14. Show students that a large angle of the blue rhombus is formed by 2 angles of the green triangles. Since each angle of a green triangle is 60°, then the large angle of the blue rhombus is 60° + 60° = 120°. The angle measures of the rhombus are 60°, 120°, 60°, and 120°.

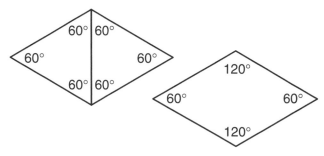

Figure 14: *Using two green triangles to find the angle measures of the blue rhombus*

Name _____ Date _____

Measuring Pattern Block Angles

The 8 pattern blocks are pictured and named. All of these shapes are polygons.

green triangle   red trapezoid   square   purple triangle

tan rhombus   blue rhombus   hexagon   brown trapezoid

1. Find the measures of the angles of the green triangle. Write the angle measures inside the pictured triangle. You may need to extend the sides.

2. Place 6 green triangles on top of the hexagon as pictured here. What is the degree measure of each of the angles of the hexagon? (*Hint:* You do not have to measure.) Write the angle measures inside the hexagon.

Angles in Triangles and Other Polygons   DAB • Grade 5 • Unit 6 • Lesson 2   **89**

Discovery Assignment Book - page 89 (Answers on p. 56)

Question 7 refers to regular polygons. **Regular polygons** have all equal sides and equal angles. Discuss this in class. The *Regular Polygons* transparency in the *Unit Resource Guide* shows several examples of both regular and nonregular polygons. Use the transparency to aid discussion. Note to students that we often mark the sides and angles to indicate congruent parts as shown in Figure 15.

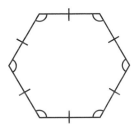

Figure 15: *Marking equal (congruent) parts of figures*

Content Note

Regular Polygons. The word regular sometimes confuses students. Remind them that words often have several meanings. Regular here does not mean "plain" or "ordinary." This is an example of a word having a very special meaning in mathematics.

On the *Regular Polygons* transparency, mark equal segments and angles. All sides and all angles of each regular shape are equal. Note that in rectangle PQRS, PQ = SR and PS = QR. All the angles are equal (right). In rhombus TUVW, all the sides are equal, and opposite angles are equal. These are illustrated in Figure 16.

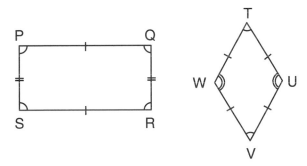

Figure 16: *Marking equal (congruent) parts*

Note that the blue rhombus has equal sides but not equal angles, so it is not a regular polygon. The green triangle, the square, and the hexagon pattern blocks are regular shapes.

To review the concepts introduced in class, students should read and complete the Angles in Polygons section of the *Angles in Triangles and Other Polygons* Activity Pages in the *Student Guide* and complete homework *Questions 1–6*.

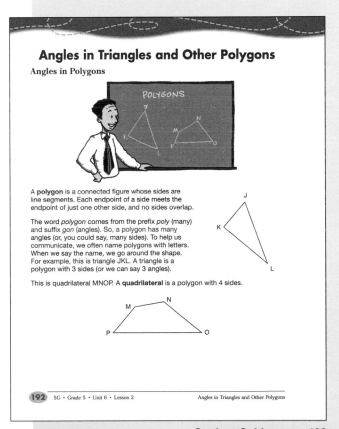

Name _____ Date _____

3. Find the angle measures for all the pattern blocks. You can use shortcuts to find angle measures.

4. Explain what shortcuts you can use to find the angle measures of the blue rhombus.

5. Explain what shortcuts you can use to find the angle measures of the red trapezoid.

6. Which of the pattern blocks are quadrilaterals?

A polygon whose sides all have equal length and whose angles all have the same degree measure is called a **regular** polygon.

7. When you lay the pattern blocks flat, the top surfaces are polygons. Which of the pattern blocks have tops that are regular polygons? Explain why.

8. Professor Peabody accidentally erased part of quadrilateral ABCD. All that is left is side BC, the bottom of the quadrilateral. See if you can redraw the quadrilateral using the following clues.

Clues:
- The measure of ∠B is 90 degrees.
- Side AB is 4 cm long.
- The measure of ∠C is 120 degrees.
- Side CD is 6 cm long.

B ———————— C

You should have enough information now to finish drawing quadrilateral ABCD.

9. ∠A = _____   10. ∠D = _____
11. AD = _____ cm

Discovery Assignment Book - page 90 (Answers on pp. 56–57)

Angles in Triangles and Other Polygons
Angles in Polygons

A **polygon** is a connected figure whose sides are line segments. Each endpoint of a side meets the endpoint of just one other side, and no sides overlap.

The word *polygon* comes from the prefix *poly* (many) and suffix *gon* (angles). So, a polygon has many angles (or, you could say, many sides). To help us communicate, we often name polygons with letters. When we say the name, we go around the shape. For example, this is triangle JKL. A triangle is a polygon with 3 sides (or we can say 3 angles).

This is quadrilateral MNOP. A **quadrilateral** is a polygon with 4 sides.

Student Guide - page 192

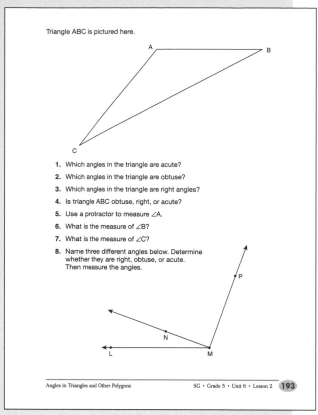

Triangle ABC is pictured here.

1. Which angles in the triangle are acute?
2. Which angles in the triangle are obtuse?
3. Which angles in the triangle are right angles?
4. Is triangle ABC obtuse, right, or acute?
5. Use a protractor to measure ∠A.
6. What is the measure of ∠B?
7. What is the measure of ∠C?
8. Name three different angles below. Determine whether they are right, obtuse, or acute. Then measure the angles.

Student Guide - page 193 (Answers on p. 53)

Adding the Angles of a Triangle
To investigate the angles in a triangle, complete the following questions.

9. Use a pencil and ruler to draw a triangle on a sheet of blank paper. Make sure the triangle covers at least one quarter of the paper.

10. Mark the vertices with dots as shown in the example.

11. Measure the three angles of the triangle with your protractor. Write the angle measures **inside** the triangle. Cut out the triangle.

12. Tear off the three angles as shown in the example.

13. On a different piece of blank paper draw a straight line. Mark a point on the line.

14. Place the three angles on the piece of paper with the drawn line. Place the angles above the line, like the pieces of a puzzle, with all the vertices touching the dot on the line.

15. What do you notice?

16. What is the sum of the three angles of your triangle?

When the corners of any triangle are torn off and placed together, they form a **straight angle.** For example, your triangle might have looked like this:

Student Guide - page 194 (Answers on p. 53)

Part 2 Adding the Angles of a Triangle

Following the directions in *Questions 9–12* in the Adding the Angles of a Triangle section in the *Student Guide,* ask students (in pairs or individually) to use a pencil and ruler to draw a triangle on a blank sheet of paper. They should make their triangles fairly large, so each one takes up at least a quarter of the paper. Then have students measure the angles, label them on the inside of the triangles, and cut out the triangles. Ask them to tear off the corners of their triangle (tear off pieces large enough to include the angle measure) as shown in Figure 17. You may wish to shade the inside of the angles as shown in Figure 17.

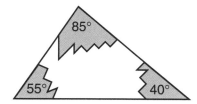

Figure 17: *An example of a triangle with its angle measures*

TIMS Tip

Make sure students tear the corner off their triangles, rather than cut them. When the corner is cut, it is harder to tell which angle was a corner of the original triangle.

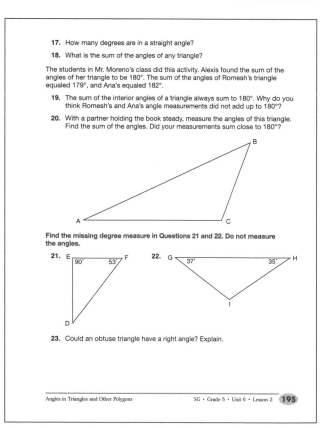

17. How many degrees are in a straight angle?
18. What is the sum of the angles of any triangle?

The students in Mr. Moreno's class did this activity. Alexis found the sum of the angles of her triangle to be 180°. The sum of the angles of Romesh's triangle equaled 179°, and Ana's equaled 182°.

19. The sum of the interior angles of a triangle always sum to 180°. Why do you think Romesh's and Ana's angle measurements did not add up to 180°?

20. With a partner holding the book steady, measure the angles of this triangle. Find the sum of the angles. Did your measurements sum close to 180°?

Find the missing degree measure in Questions 21 and 22. Do not measure the angles.

21.
22.

23. Could an obtuse triangle have a right angle? Explain.

Student Guide - page 195 (Answers on p. 54)

On another sheet of paper, ask students to draw a line and mark a point on the line *(Question 13)*. Have children place all three corners on the same side of the line, corners meeting at the point as in Figure 18. Ask students what they notice *(Question 15)*. They should find that the corners fit exactly on one side of the line with no gaps or overlaps, indicating that the interior sum of the angles of their triangle is 180°, i.e., a straight angle. Have them check this by adding the measures they found *(Question 16)*. Most students will probably get a sum that is close to, but not equal to, 180 degrees. Since students drew many different triangles and for all them the sum of the angles was 180° (or close to 180°), it is reasonably certain that the sum of the angles of all triangles is 180°. Ask:

- *Why did some students' angle measurements not add up to exactly 180°?* (One possibility, of course, is that they did not measure very well. But even with a lot of careful work, measurements are not exact. Factors that contribute to inaccuracy in measuring angles include imprecise tools, i.e., protractors, and the thickness of the lines of the triangle we are measuring. These are unavoidable. To be off a degree or two on an angle is acceptable.)

Discuss the discrepancies. By the end of the discussion, however, students should understand that if measured precisely, the sum of the angles of every triangle is 180 degrees.

Ask students to complete the Adding the Angles of a Triangle section of the *Angles in Triangles and Other Polygons* Activity Pages in the *Student Guide*. *Question 23* asks whether a triangle could have an obtuse angle and a right angle. Some students will be able to argue that this is impossible since an obtuse angle measures more than 90°, the obtuse angle and the right angle together already give a sum greater than 180°. You can assign Homework *Questions 7–9.*

Math Facts

DPP item E provides practice with the last six facts. Item G introduces the fact families for the last six facts.

Homework and Practice

- Assign DPP Tasks F and H, which review area and fractions.
- Students can complete Homework *Questions 1–6* on the *Angles in Triangles and Other Polygons* Activity Pages in the *Student Guide* after Part 1. They will need protractors to complete the homework.

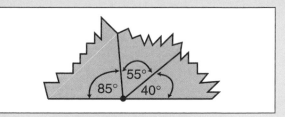

Figure 18: *Illustrating that the angle measures of a triangle sum to 180 degrees*

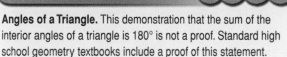

Angles of a Triangle. This demonstration that the sum of the interior angles of a triangle is 180° is not a proof. Standard high school geometry textbooks include a proof of this statement.

TIMS Tip

Students will use the quadrilateral and pentagon they draw in *Questions 8–9* in Lesson 3.

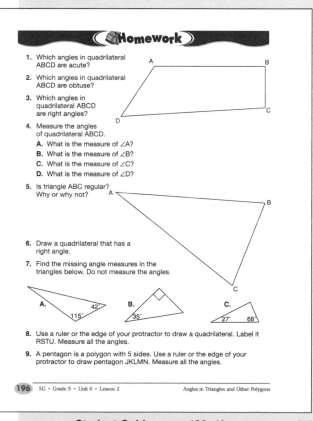

Student Guide - page 196 *(Answers on p. 54)*

Unit 6 Home Practice

PART 1 Triangle Flash Cards: Last Six Facts

Study for the quiz on the multiplication and division facts for the last six facts (4×6, 4×7, 4×8, 6×7, 6×8, and 7×8). Take home your *Triangle Flash Cards: Last Six Facts* and your list of facts you need to study.

Ask a family member to choose one flash card at a time. To quiz you on a multiplication fact, he or she should cover the corner containing the highest number. Multiply the two uncovered numbers.

To quiz you on a division fact, your family member can cover one of the smaller numbers. One of the smaller numbers is circled. The other has a square around it. Use the two uncovered numbers to solve a division fact.

Ask your family member to mix up the multiplication and division facts. He or she should sometimes cover the highest number, sometimes cover the circled number, and sometimes cover the number in the square.

Your teacher will tell you when the quiz on the last six facts will be given.

PART 2 Practicing Addition and Subtraction

Use paper and pencil to solve the following problems. Estimate to be sure your answers are reasonable. Use a separate sheet of paper, if you need more work space.

A. $549 + 82 =$ _____   B. $629 - 347 =$ _____   C. $843 + 178 =$ _____

D. $213 - 58 =$ _____   E. $7542 + 282 =$ _____   F. $1067 + 93 =$ _____

G. $4057 - 492 =$ _____   H. $2715 + 206 =$ _____   I. $462 - 379 =$ _____

GEOMETRY   DAB • Grade 5 • Unit 6   **81**

Discovery Assignment Book - page 81 (Answers on p. 55)

PART 3 Angles and Triangles

You will need a protractor to complete this section. Use the straight edge on your protractor to draw the angles and triangle in Questions 1, 2, and 4.

1. On a separate sheet of paper, draw an angle that is greater than 90°. Name the angle YTV. Then measure the angle to the nearest degree.

2. On a separate sheet of paper, draw an angle that is less than 45°. Name the angle RGM. Then measure the angle to the nearest degree.

3. If triangle ADK has two angles that are 40° each, what is the measure of the third angle? How do you know?

4. Can a triangle have two 70° angles and one that measures 50°? How do you know?

5. One angle in triangle QFP is a right angle. A second angle is 27°. What is the measure of the third angle? How do you know?

6. One angle in a triangle measures 32°. Another angle is twice as large. What is the measure of the third angle? How do you know?

PART 4 Practicing Multiplication and Division

Use paper and pencil to solve the following problems. Estimate to be sure your answers are reasonable. Use a separate sheet of paper to show your work.

A. $607 \times 8 =$ _____   B. $174 \times 9 =$ _____   C. $435 \div 3 =$ _____

D. $420 \div 9 =$ _____   E. $4631 \times 5 =$ _____   F. $768 \div 5 =$ _____

G. $68 \times 34 =$ _____   H. $577 \div 7 =$ _____   I. $1652 \div 4 =$ _____

82   DAB • Grade 5 • Unit 6   GEOMETRY

Discovery Assignment Book - page 82 (Answers on p. 55)

- You can assign Homework *Questions 7–9* for homework after Part 2. *Questions 8–9* ask students to draw a quadrilateral and a pentagon and then measure the angles. These figures can be used in the class investigation described in Lesson 3.

- Assign Parts 2 and 3 of the Home Practice. Part 2 practices addition and subtraction. Part 3 explores angles and triangles.

Answers for Parts 2 and 3 of the Home Practice are in the Answer Key at the end of this lesson and at the end of this unit.

Assessment

- You can use DPP Bit M from an upcoming lesson as a quiz. This item asks students to use what they have learned in this lesson to find the measures of the angles of four different triangles.

- Use the *Observational Assessment Record* to document students' abilities to identify, describe, and classify 2D shapes.

At a Glance

Math Facts and Daily Practice and Problems

Complete DPP items E–H for this lesson. Item E provides practice with the last six facts. Item G introduces fact families.

Part 1. Angles in Polygons

1. Draw a quadrilateral and measure the angles together as a class.
2. Define polygons.
3. Define quadrilateral as a polygon with four sides.
4. Discuss how to name quadrilaterals with letters.
5. Students complete the *Measuring Pattern Block Angles* Activity Pages in the *Discovery Assignment Book.*
6. Discuss regular polygons using the *Regular Polygons* transparency in the *Unit Resource Guide.*
7. Students complete *Questions 1–8* in the *Student Guide.*

Part 2. Adding the Angles of a Triangle

1. Students follow the directions in the *Student Guide (Questions 9–11).* They draw a triangle, measure its angles, label each angle with its measure, and cut it out.
2. Students tear off the corners of the triangle and place the vertices at a point on a line to show they form a straight angle. They find the sum of the measures of the angles. *(Questions 12–16)*
3. Discuss with students that the sum of the interior angles of a triangle is 180°. *(Questions 17–23)*

Homework

1. Assign *Questions 1–6* in the Homework section of the *Student Guide* after Part 1.
2. Assign *Questions 7–9* in the Homework section after Part 2.
3. Assign Parts 2 and 3 of the Home Practice.

Assessment

1. Use DPP item M as an assessment.
2. Use the *Observational Assessment Record* to document students' abilities to identify, describe, and classify 2D shapes.

Answer Key is on pages 53–57.

Notes:

Regular Polygons

These polygons are regular.

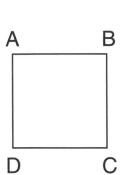

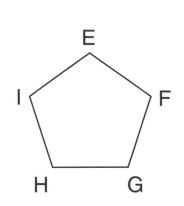

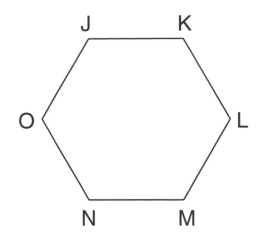

These polygons are not regular.

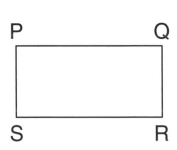

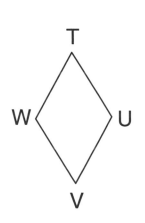

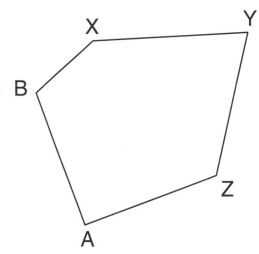

Transparency Master

Student Guide (p. 193)

1. ∠B and ∠C

2. ∠A

3. none

4. obtuse

5. 129°

6. 28°

7. 23°

8. ∠LMN, ∠LMP, and ∠PMN; ∠LMN (20°) is acute, ∠LMP is obtuse (110°), and ∠PMN (90°) is a right angle.

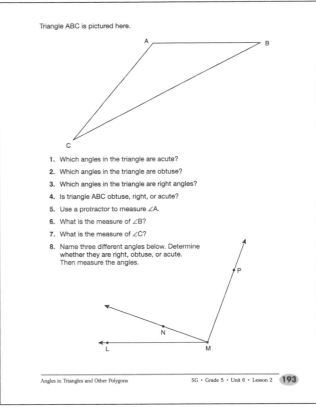

Triangle ABC is pictured here.

1. Which angles in the triangle are acute?
2. Which angles in the triangle are obtuse?
3. Which angles in the triangle are right angles?
4. Is triangle ABC obtuse, right, or acute?
5. Use a protractor to measure ∠A.
6. What is the measure of ∠B?
7. What is the measure of ∠C?
8. Name three different angles below. Determine whether they are right, obtuse, or acute. Then measure the angles.

Angles in Triangles and Other Polygons   SG • Grade 5 • Unit 6 • Lesson 2   **193**

Student Guide - page 193

Student Guide (p. 194)

9.–14. See Figures 17 and 18 in Lesson Guide 2 for an example.

15. The three angles fit exactly on one side of the line. They form a straight angle.*

16. 180° or close to 180°*

Adding the Angles of a Triangle
To investigate the angles in a triangle, complete the following questions.

9. Use a pencil and ruler to draw a triangle on a sheet of blank paper. Make sure the triangle covers at least one quarter of the paper.

10. Mark the vertices with dots as shown in the example.

11. Measure the three angles of the triangle with your protractor. Write the angle measures **inside** the triangle. Cut out the triangle.

12. Tear off the three angles as shown in the example.

13. On a different piece of blank paper draw a straight line. Mark a point on the line.

14. Place the three angles on the piece of paper with the drawn line. Place the angles above the line, like the pieces of a puzzle, with all the vertices touching the dot on the line.

15. What do you notice?

16. What is the sum of the three angles of your triangle?

When the corners of any triangle are torn off and placed together, they form a **straight angle.** For example, your triangle might have looked like this:

85°
55°   40°

55°
85°   40°

194 SG • Grade 5 • Unit 6 • Lesson 2   Angles in Triangles and Other Polygons

Student Guide - page 194

*Answers and/or discussion are included in the Lesson Guide.

17. How many degrees are in a straight angle?

18. What is the sum of the angles of any triangle?

The students in Mr. Moreno's class did this activity. Alexis found the sum of the angles of her triangle to be 180°. The sum of the angles of Romesh's triangle equaled 179°, and Ana's equaled 182°.

19. The sum of the interior angles of a triangle always sum to 180°. Why do you think Romesh's and Ana's angle measurements did not add to 180°?

20. With a partner holding the book steady, measure the angles of this triangle. Find the sum of the angles. Did your measurements sum close to 180°?

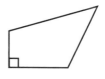

Find the missing degree measure in Questions 21 and 22. Do not measure the angles.

21.   22.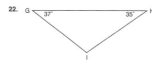

23. Could an obtuse triangle have a right angle? Explain.

Angles in Triangles and Other Polygons   SG • Grade 5 • Unit 6 • Lesson 2   **195**

Student Guide - page 195

Student Guide (p. 195)

17. 180°

18. 180°

19. The protractor is not accurate or the line is too thick.

20. ∠A = 25°; ∠B = 45°; ∠C = 110°

21. 37°

22. 108°

23. No*

Student Guide (p. 196)

Homework

1. ∠D

2. ∠A and ∠C

3. ∠B

4. **A.** ∠A = 124°   **C.** ∠C = 94°
   B. ∠B = 90°   **D.** ∠D = 52°

5. No. The three sides are not the same measurement. The three angles are not the same measurement.

6. Shapes will vary.
   Make sure the shape has four sides and at least one right angle. An example is shown here.

7. **A.** 23°   **B.** 55°   **C.** 85°

8. Shapes will vary.

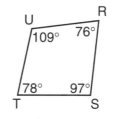

9. Shapes will vary.

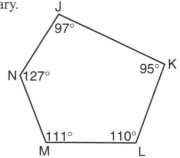

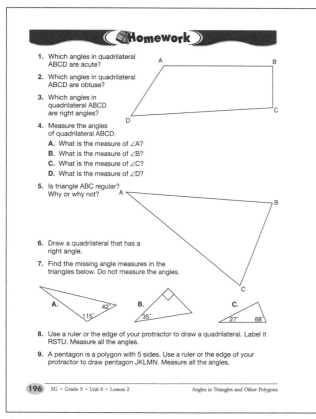

Student Guide - page 196

Discovery Assignment Book (p. 81)

Home Practice*

Part 2. Practicing Addition and Subtraction

A. 631

B. 282

C. 1021

D. 155

E. 7824

F. 1160

G. 3565

H. 2921

I. 83

Name _____ Date _____

Unit 6 Home Practice

PART 1 *Triangle Flash Cards: Last Six Facts*
Study for the quiz on the multiplication and division facts for the last six facts (4×6, 4×7, 4×8, 6×7, 6×8, and 7×8). Take home your *Triangle Flash Cards: Last Six Facts* and your list of facts you need to study.

Ask a family member to choose one flash card at a time. To quiz you on a multiplication fact, he or she should cover the corner containing the highest number. Multiply the two uncovered numbers.

To quiz you on a division fact, your family member can cover one of the smaller numbers. One of the smaller numbers is circled. The other has a square around it. Use the two uncovered numbers to solve a division fact.

Ask your family member to mix up the multiplication and division facts. He or she should sometimes cover the highest number, sometimes cover the circled number, and sometimes cover the number in the square.

Your teacher will tell you when the quiz on the last six facts will be given.

PART 2 Practicing Addition and Subtraction
Use paper and pencil to solve the following problems. Estimate to be sure your answers are reasonable. Use a separate sheet of paper, if you need more work space.

A. $549 + 82 =$ _____   B. $629 - 347 =$ _____   C. $843 + 178 =$ _____

D. $213 - 58 =$ _____   E. $7542 + 282 =$ _____   F. $1067 + 93 =$ _____

G. $4057 - 492 =$ _____   H. $2715 + 206 =$ _____   I. $462 - 379 =$ _____

GEOMETRY   DAB • Grade 5 • Unit 6   **81**

Discovery Assignment Book - page 81

Discovery Assignment Book (p. 82)

Part 3. Angles and Triangles

I. Angles will vary. One possible angle is shown.

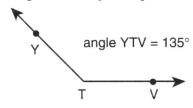

angle YTV = 135°

2. Angles will vary. One possible angle is shown.

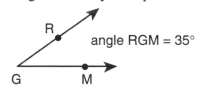

angle RGM = 35°

3. 100°; 40° + 40° = 80°; 180° − 80° = 100°.

4. No. 70° + 70° + 50° = 190°.

5. 180° − 27° − 90° = 63°.

6. 32° + (32° × 2) = 96°; 180° − 96° = 84°.

Name _____ Date _____

PART 3 Angles and Triangles
You will need a protractor to complete this section. Use the straight edge on your protractor to draw the angles and triangle in Questions 1, 2, and 4.

1. On a separate sheet of paper, draw an angle that is greater than 90°. Name the angle YTV. Then measure the angle to the nearest degree.

2. On a separate sheet of paper, draw an angle that is less than 45°. Name the angle RGM. Then measure the angle to the nearest degree.

3. If triangle ADK has two angles that are 40° each, what is the measure of the third angle? How do you know?

4. Can a triangle have two 70° angles and one that measures 50°? How do you know?

5. One angle in triangle QFP is a right angle. A second angle is 27°. What is the measure of the third angle? How do you know?

6. One angle in a triangle measures 32°. Another angle is twice as large. What is the measure of the third angle? How do you know?

PART 4 Practicing Multiplication and Division
Use paper and pencil to solve the following problems. Estimate to be sure your answers are reasonable. Use a separate sheet of paper to show your work.

A. $607 \times 8 =$ _____   B. $174 \times 9 =$ _____   C. $435 \div 3 =$ _____

D. $420 \div 9 =$ _____   E. $4631 \times 5 =$ _____   F. $768 \div 5 =$ _____

G. $68 \times 34 =$ _____   H. $577 \div 7 =$ _____   I. $1652 \div 4 =$ _____

82 DAB • Grade 5 • Unit 6   GEOMETRY

Discovery Assignment Book - page 82

---

*Answers for all the Home Practice in the *Discovery Assignment Book* are at the end of the unit.

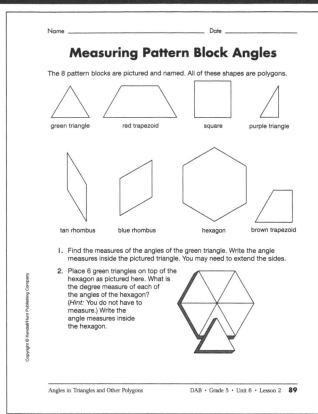

Discovery Assignment Book - page 89

Discovery Assignment Book (pp. 89–90)

Measuring Pattern Block Angles

1.–3.

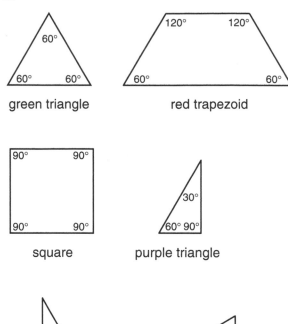

green triangle   red trapezoid

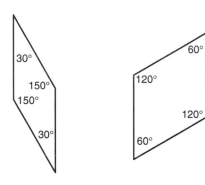

square   purple triangle

tan rhombus   blue rhombus

hexagon   brown trapezoid

4.   See Figure 14 in Lesson Guide 2.*

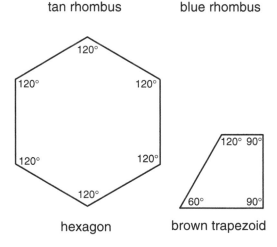

Name _____ Date _____

3. Find the angle measures for all the pattern blocks. You can use shortcuts to find angle measures.

4. Explain what shortcuts you can use to find the angle measures of the blue rhombus.

5. Explain what shortcuts you can use to find the angle measures of the red trapezoid.

6. Which of the pattern blocks are quadrilaterals?

A polygon whose sides all have equal length and whose angles all have the same degree measure is called a **regular** polygon.

7. When you lay the pattern blocks flat, the top surfaces are polygons. Which of the pattern blocks have tops that are regular polygons? Explain why.

8. Professor Peabody accidentally erased part of quadrilateral ABCD. All that is left is side BC, the bottom of the quadrilateral. See if you can redraw the quadrilateral using the following clues.

   Clues:
   • The measure of ∠B is 90 degrees.
   • Side AB is 4 cm long.
   • The measure of ∠C is 120 degrees.
   • Side CD is 6 cm long.

B   C

You should have enough information now to finish drawing quadrilateral ABCD.

9. ∠A = _____   10. ∠D = _____

11. AD = _____ cm

Discovery Assignment Book - page 90

*Answers and/or discussion are included in the Lesson Guide.

5. By placing three green triangles on top of the red trapezoid you can see that two of the trapezoid's angles are 60° and the other two are 120°.

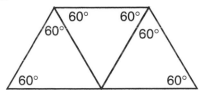

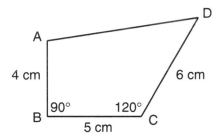

6. red trapezoid, square, tan rhombus, blue rhombus, and brown trapezoid

7. green triangle, square, and hexagon

8.

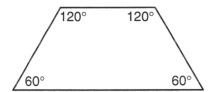

9. ∠A = 99°

10. ∠D = 51°

11. AD = 8.1 cm

Lesson 3

Polygon Angles

Students discover a relationship between the number of sides of a polygon and the sum of the angles. While discovering this pattern, students review or learn the names of many polygons and how to triangulate a polygon.

Key Content

- Investigating, describing, and reasoning about the results of subdividing polygons.
- Finding patterns in the sum of angles of polygons.
- Investigating properties of regular polygons.
- Making and testing conjectures about geometric properties.
- Using numerical variables.
- Expressing mathematical relationships using formulas.

Key Vocabulary

- decagon
- diagonal
- dodecagon
- equilateral triangle
- hexagon
- *N*-gon
- nonagon
- octagon
- pentagon
- regular polygon
- septagon
- triangulating

Homework

1. Students can complete the homework problems in the *Polygon Angles* Activity Pages in the *Student Guide* after completing the *Polygon Angles Data Table.*
2. Assign Part 4 of the Home Practice.

Assessment

Use the Journal Prompt as assessment.

Materials List

Supplies and Copies

Student	Teacher
Supplies for Each Student • calculator • protractor • ruler	**Supplies** • protractor
Copies	**Copies/Transparencies** • 1 transparency of *Polygon Angles Data Table*, optional (*Discovery Assignment Book* Page 91)

All blackline masters including assessment, transparency, and DPP masters are also on the Teacher Resource CD.

Student Books
Polygon Angles (*Student Guide* Pages 197–200)
Polygon Angles Data Table (*Discovery Assignment Book* Page 91)

Daily Practice and Problems and Home Practice
DPP items I–J (*Unit Resource Guide* Pages 20–21)
Home Practice Part 4 (*Discovery Assignment Book* Page 82)

Note: Classrooms whose pacing differs significantly from the suggested pacing of the units should use the Math Facts Calendar in Section 4 of the *Facts Resource Guide* to ensure students receive the complete math facts program.

I. Bit: Practice (URG p. 20)

1. Estimate the answers to the following problems. Be ready to share your strategies with the class.

   A. $17 \times 56 =$ B. $1674 \div 4 =$

   C. $43 \times 77 =$

2. Solve the following problems using a paper-and-pencil method. Estimate to be sure your answers are reasonable.

   A. $870 \div 6 =$ B. $7045 \div 8 =$

   C. $34 \times 56 =$

J. Challenge: Sale! (URG p. 21)

The local department store is having a "10 percent off everything" sale.

   A. About how much will a customer save on each item listed below?

   B. Estimate the cost of each item on sale.

1. t-shirts are regularly $12.50 each
2. blue jeans are regularly $29.97 each
3. sweat shirts are regularly $22.50 each
4. jackets are regularly $67.40 each
5. sweaters are regularly $19.95 each

Students drew their own quadrilaterals and pentagons as homework for Lesson 2, *Questions 8–9* in the *Student Guide*. They can use these two figures for the investigation in this lesson.

Ask students to draw a quadrilateral and measure the angles (they may have done this for homework). Have students find the sum of the interior angles and report the sum to the class. The sums should be close to 360°. If not, have them check their work within the groups. Ask the class:

- *All of you drew different quadrilaterals. Why is the sum of all the angles always 360°?*

Sometimes, a child will make the connection to the fact that the angles of a triangle add up to 180°. Other times, you may have to suggest they draw a diagonal. Remind them that a **diagonal** in a polygon is a line segment that connects nonadjacent corners. Note there are always two different ways to draw a diagonal in a quadrilateral. Ask the following:

- *What do you see after drawing the diagonal?* (The diagonal partitions the quadrilateral into two nonoverlapping triangles. This is called **triangulating** a polygon.)

- *What do you know about the angles of triangles?* (Eventually, the class will deduce that since the sum of the angles of a triangle is 180 degrees and there are two triangles with nonoverlapping angles in a quadrilateral, the sum of the angles of a quadrilateral must be 360°.)

An example is shown in Figure 19. The first page of the *Polygon Angles* Activity Pages in the *Student Guide* discusses and illustrates triangulating a quadrilateral as well. Have students read and answer *Questions 1–4.*

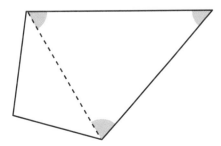

Figure 19: *A triangulated quadrilateral*

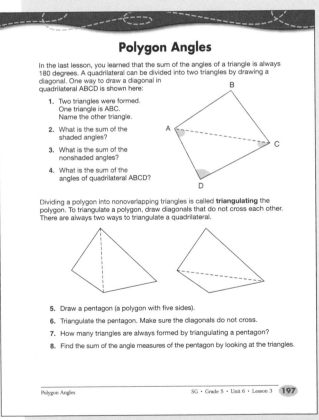

Polygon Angles

In the last lesson, you learned that the sum of the angles of a triangle is always 180 degrees. A quadrilateral can be divided into two triangles by drawing a diagonal. One way to draw a diagonal in quadrilateral ABCD is shown here:

1. Two triangles were formed. One triangle is ABC. Name the other triangle.

2. What is the sum of the shaded angles?

3. What is the sum of the nonshaded angles?

4. What is the sum of the angles of quadrilateral ABCD?

Dividing a polygon into nonoverlapping triangles is called **triangulating** the polygon. To triangulate a polygon, draw diagonals that do not cross each other. There are always two ways to triangulate a quadrilateral.

5. Draw a pentagon (a polygon with five sides).

6. Triangulate the pentagon. Make sure the diagonals do not cross.

7. How many triangles are always formed by triangulating a pentagon?

8. Find the sum of the angle measures of the pentagon by looking at the triangles.

Polygon Angles   SG • Grade 5 • Unit 6 • Lesson 3 **197**

Student Guide - page 197 (Answers on p. 67)

The names of the polygons in the table below are of Latin or Greek origin. Many English words use the same prefixes. For example, a **tri**angle is a polygon with three sides or angles. A **tri**cycle is a vehicle with three wheels. A **tri**logy is a story in three parts. The 11-sided polygon does not have a name that is commonly used. This is also true for most polygons that have greater than 12 sides.

Polygon Name	Number of Sides/Angles
triangle	3
quadrilateral	4
pentagon	5
hexagon	6
septagon	7
octagon	8
nonagon	9
decagon	10
dodecagon	12

9. Use the *Polygon Angles Data Table* Activity Page in the *Discovery Assignment Book*. Fill in the rows for the triangle, quadrilateral, and pentagon. Leave the last column blank. Your *Polygon Angles Data Table* should look like this:

Polygon	Number of Sides	Number of Angles	Number of Triangles	Sum of Angles (degrees)	Measure of One Angle of a Regular Polygon (degrees)
triangle	3	3	1	180	
quadrilateral	4	4	2	360	

Student Guide - page 198 *(Answers on p. 67)*

Name _____ Date _____

Polygon Angles Data Table

Fill in the rows for the triangle, quadrilateral, and pentagon. Leave the last column blank. Then complete the table through the dodecagon (12-sided polygon). Your class will discuss the entries for the final column and last row.

Polygon	Number of Sides	Number of Angles	Number of Triangles	Sum of Angles (degrees)	Measure of One Angle of a Regular Polygon (degrees)
triangle					
quadrilateral					
pentagon					
hexagon					
septagon					
octagon					
nonagon					
decagon					
11-gon					
dodecagon					
N-gon					

Discovery Assignment Book - page 91 *(Answers on p. 69)*

Questions 5–8 in the *Student Guide* discuss triangulating a pentagon. Make sure students triangulate their pentagons correctly; that is, without overlapping diagonals. See Figure 20 for correct and incorrect solutions. Since a pentagon can be divided into 3 triangles, the sum of the interior angles of a pentagon is $3 \times 180 = 540°$.

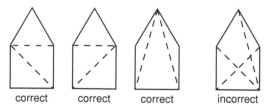

correct   correct   correct   incorrect

Figure 20: *Correct and incorrect triangulations of a pentagon*

To continue investigating the angles of polygons, ask students to read the *Polygon Angles* Activity Pages in the *Student Guide* and use the *Polygon Angles Data Table* Activity Page in the *Discovery Assignment Book*. Allow them to work in groups, following the instructions on the pages ***(Questions 9–16)***.

Double check that students understand that when they dissect a polygon into triangles (triangulate a polygon), the triangles must not overlap. For example, two ways to triangulate a hexagon are shown in Figure 21.

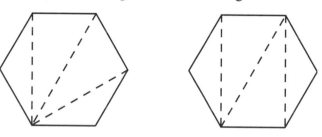

Figure 21: *Two ways to triangulate a hexagon*

TIMS Tip

Discuss the names of the polygons. Learning the prefixes will aid students in understanding many other words. You might encourage them to find other words with these prefixes as part of language study. For example, what do the following words mean?

- octogenarian—between 80 and 90 years of age or a person between 80 and 90 years of age.
- triplets—a set of three or a set of three babies born at the same time.
- decade—a period of ten years.
- hexapod—having six legs or feet.

Encourage students to talk among themselves about any patterns they see in the chart. For example, they may see that as the number of sides increases, the number of ways to triangulate grows. They may also see that as the number of sides increases by one, the number of triangles increases by 1 and the sum of the angles increases by 180°.

Question 10 asks children to complete the chart except for the last row and last column. As they work, encourage them to look for patterns, to make predictions, and then to check them. Remind students that if they are certain of an entry in the table, they need not do the computations. Make sure all groups fill in the table correctly. See Figure 22.

The last row generalizes the pattern *(Questions 11–13)*. The general pattern can be described in words or using symbols. Ask students to generalize the patterns in their own words first. One way to describe the general pattern in words is to say "The number of triangles is two less than the number of sides, so we multiply that number by 180° to get the sum of the angles." To say the same thing in symbols, we can say, "If N is the number of sides, then $N - 2$ is the number of triangles and $180 \times (N - 2)$ is the sum of the angles *(S)*. So, $S = 180 \times (N - 2)$.

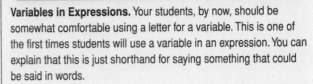
Remind students that in a **regular polygon** every angle must have the same measure and every side must be the same length. Review **Question 14** with students. Make sure they understand that since a square has 4 angles and they must be equal, then to find the degree measure of each, they must divide 360 by 4. Similarly, for **Question 15,** since the sum of the angles of a triangle is 180, then $180 \div 3$ gives 60 degrees for each angle of a regular triangle or equilateral triangle. Have students continue to fill in the final column in the table *(Question 16)*. Check their entries.

The completed *Polygon Angles Data Table* is shown in Figure 22.

Polygon	Number of Sides	Number of Angles	Number of Triangles	Sum of Angles (degrees)	Measure of One Angle of a Regular Polygon (degrees)
triangle	3	3	1	180	60
quadrilateral	4	4	2	360	90
pentagon	5	5	3	540	108
hexagon	6	6	4	720	120
septagon	7	7	5	900	128.6
octagon	8	8	6	1080	135
nonagon	9	9	7	1260	140
decagon	10	10	8	1440	144
11-gon	11	11	9	1620	147.3
dodecagon	12	12	10	1800	150
N-gon	N	N	$N - 2$	$180 \times (N-2)$	$\dfrac{180 \times (N-2)}{N}$

Figure 22: *Polygon Angles Data Table*

Student Guide - page 199 (Answers on p. 68)

10. Fill in the *Polygon Angles Data Table* through dodecagon (a 12-sided polygon) by triangulating the polygons. Do not fill in the last column yet. Look for patterns.

When mathematicians talk about an *N*-gon, they mean a polygon that has *N* sides, where *N* is a whole number.

11. How many angles does an *N*-gon have? Record this in the table.

12. Look at the patterns. Predict how many triangles are formed when an *N*-gon is triangulated. Record this in the table.

13. By looking at the pattern, predict the sum of the angles of an *N*-gon. Record this in the table.

A polygon is **regular** if all sides are the same length *and* all angles have the same degree measure.

regular quadrilateral

regular triangle

14. A square is a special quadrilateral.
   A. What is the sum of the angles in a square?
   B. Since all the angles of a square are equal, what is the measure of each angle? How do you know?

An equilateral triangle is regular because all its sides are the same length and all its angles are equal.

15. What is the measure of any angle of an equilateral triangle?

16. Fill in the remaining column in the *Polygon Angles Data Table*.

Polygon Angles   SG • Grade 5 • Unit 6 • Lesson 3 **199**

Student Guide - page 200 (Answers on p. 68)

Homework

Use your completed *Polygon Angles Data Table* to help you complete these problems.

1. Three of the angles of a quadrilateral have angle measures of 59°, 136°, and 89°. What is the measure of the remaining angle?

2. Four of the angles of a pentagon have angle measures of 74°, 120°, 138°, and 143°. What is the measure of the remaining angle?

3. Two angles of a hexagon have equal measure. The other angles have measures of 83°, 97°, 126°, and 98°. How many degrees are each of the two remaining angles?

4. A. Draw an octagon.
   B. Find two different ways of triangulating the octagon. Use different colored pencils or pens to help you.
   C. How many triangles are formed when an octagon is triangulated?
   D. What is the sum of the angles of an octagon?

What do you call a lost parrot?
A "polygon."

5. A. What is the sum of the angles in degrees of a regular 15-gon (a polygon with 15 sides)?
   B. What is the measure of one angle of a regular 15-gon?

6. A. What is the sum of the angles in degrees of a regular 20-gon?
   B. What is the measure of one angle of a regular 20-gon?

200 SG • Grade 5 • Unit 6 • Lesson 3   Polygon Angles

Homework and Practice

- You can assign *Questions 1–4* in the Homework section on the *Polygon Angles* Activity Pages after students complete the *Polygon Data Table* through the hexagon row. Assign *Questions 5–6* when the table is complete.

- Use DPP Bit I to practice estimation and paper-and-pencil computation with multiplication and division.

- Assign Part 4 of the Home Practice, which provides practice with paper-and-pencil multiplication and division.

Answers for Part 4 of the Home Practice are in the Answer Key at the end of this lesson and at the end of this unit.

Assessment

Use the Journal Prompt to assess students' abilities to communicate their understanding of the concepts in the lesson.

Journal Prompt

Explain why the angles of a quadrilateral sum to 360 degrees.

Name _____ Date _____

PART 3 Angles and Triangles
You will need a protractor to complete this section. Use the straight edge on your protractor to draw the angles and triangle in Questions 1, 2, and 4.

1. On a separate sheet of paper, draw an angle that is greater than 90°. Name the angle YTV. Then measure the angle to the nearest degree.

2. On a separate sheet of paper, draw an angle that is less than 45°. Name the angle RGM. Then measure the angle to the nearest degree.

3. If triangle ADK has two angles that are 40° each, what is the measure of the third angle? How do you know?

4. Can a triangle have two 70° angles and one that measures 50°? How do you know?

5. One angle in triangle QFP is a right angle. A second angle is 27°. What is the measure of the third angle? How do you know?

6. One angle in a triangle measures 32°. Another angle is twice as large. What is the measure of the third angle? How do you know?

PART 4 Practicing Multiplication and Division
Use paper and pencil to solve the following problems. Estimate to be sure your answers are reasonable. Use a separate sheet of paper to show your work.

A. $607 \times 8 =$ _____   B. $174 \times 9 =$ _____   C. $435 \div 3 =$ _____

D. $420 \div 9 =$ _____   E. $4631 \times 5 =$ _____   F. $768 \div 5 =$ _____

G. $68 \times 34 =$ _____   H. $577 \div 7 =$ _____   I. $1652 \div 4 =$ _____

82 DAB • Grade 5 • Unit 6   GEOMETRY

Discovery Assignment Book - page 82 (Answers on p. 69)

- Assign DPP Challenge J as a review of finding 10%. Assign this item only if students completed Unit 4 Lesson 4 *How Close Is Close Enough?*

- As a language arts connection, ask students to find more words that begin with the prefixes they used in this lesson. You can also have students investigate the origins of these prefixes.

Content Note

September and October. Your students might realize that the prefixes *sept* and *oct* appear in September and October. This seems puzzling since they are the ninth and tenth months of the year. In the early days of the Roman civilization, they were the seventh and eighth months. Later, July was added in honor of Julius Caesar and August was added in honor of Augustus Caesar.

At a Glance

Math Facts and Daily Practice and Problems

Complete DPP items I–J for this lesson.

Teaching the Activity

1. Students measure the interior angles of a quadrilateral.
2. Students divide the quadrilateral into 2 triangles to see that the sum of the angles of a quadrilateral must equal 360°. Students complete *Questions 1–4* in the *Student Guide.*
3. Students learn to triangulate a polygon. *(Questions 5–8)*
4. Students complete the *Polygon Angles Data Table* Activity Page in the *Discovery Assignment Book* through dodecagons by following the discussion in the *Polygon Angles* Activity Pages in the *Student Guide. (Questions 9–10)*
5. Students generalize the sum of the angles of an *N*-gon to be $180 \times (N - 2)$. *(Questions 11–13)*
6. Students find the angles of the regular polygons in the *Polygon Angles Data Table* and complete the last column of the table. *(Questions 5–8)*

Homework

1. Have students complete the homework problems in the *Polygon Angles* Activity Pages in the *Student Guide* after completing the *Polygon Angles* Data Table.
2. Assign Part 4 of the Home Practice.

Assessment

Use the Journal Prompt as an assessment.

Extension

1. Assign DPP Challenge J.
2. Challenge students to find more words that begin with the prefixes used in this lesson.

Answer Key is on pages 67–69.

Notes:

Student Guide (p. 197)

Polygon Angles

1. triangle ACD

2. 180°

3. 180°

4. 360°

5.–6. See Figure 20 in Lesson Guide 3.*

7. 3 triangles

8. 540°

Polygon Angles

In the last lesson, you learned that the sum of the angles of a triangle is always 180 degrees. A quadrilateral can be divided into two triangles by drawing a diagonal. One way to draw a diagonal in quadrilateral ABCD is shown here:

1. Two triangles were formed. One triangle is ABC. Name the other triangle.

2. What is the sum of the shaded angles?

3. What is the sum of the nonshaded angles?

4. What is the sum of the angles of quadrilateral ABCD?

Dividing a polygon into nonoverlapping triangles is called **triangulating** the polygon. To triangulate a polygon, draw diagonals that do not cross each other. There are always two ways to triangulate a quadrilateral.

5. Draw a pentagon (a polygon with five sides).

6. Triangulate the pentagon. Make sure the diagonals do not cross.

7. How many triangles are always formed by triangulating a pentagon?

8. Find the sum of the angle measures of the pentagon by looking at the triangles.

Polygon Angles   SG • Grade 5 • Unit 6 • Lesson 3   197

Student Guide - page 197

Student Guide (p. 198)

9. See Figure 22 in Lesson Guide 3 for a completed data table.*

The names of the polygons in the table below are of Latin or Greek origin. Many English words use the same prefixes. For example, a **tri**angle is a polygon with three sides or angles. A **tri**cycle is a vehicle with three wheels. A **tri**logy is a story in three parts. The 11-sided polygon does not have a name that is commonly used. This is also true for most polygons that have greater than 12 sides.

Polygon Name	Number of Sides/Angles
triangle	3
quadrilateral	4
pentagon	5
hexagon	6
septagon	7
octagon	8
nonagon	9
decagon	10
dodecagon	12

9. Use the *Polygon Angles Data Table* Activity Page in the *Discovery Assignment Book*. Fill in the rows for the triangle, quadrilateral, and pentagon. Leave the last column blank. Your *Polygon Angles Data Table* should look like this:

Polygon	Number of Sides	Number of Angles	Number of Triangles	Sum of Angles (degrees)	Measure of One Angle of a Regular Polygon (degrees)
triangle	3	3	1	180	
quadrilateral	4	4	2	360	

198   SG • Grade 5 • Unit 6 • Lesson 3   Polygon Angles

Student Guide - page 198

*Answers and/or discussion are included in the Lesson Guide.

Student Guide (p. 199)

10. Fill in the *Polygon Angles Data Table* through dodecagon (a 12-sided polygon) by triangulating the polygons. Do not fill in the last column yet. Look for patterns.

When mathematicians talk about an *N*-gon, they mean a polygon that has *N* sides, where *N* is a whole number.

11. How many angles does an *N*-gon have? Record this in the table.

12. Look at the patterns. Predict how many triangles are formed when an *N*-gon is triangulated. Record this in the table.

13. By looking at the pattern, predict the sum of the angles of an *N*-gon. Record this in the table.

A polygon is **regular** if all sides are the same length *and* all angles have the same degree measure.

regular quadrilateral   regular triangle

14. A square is a special quadrilateral.
   A. What is the sum of the angles in a square?
   B. Since all the angles of a square are equal, what is the measure of each angle? How do you know?

An equilateral triangle is regular because all its sides are the same length and all its angles are equal.

15. What is the measure of any angle of an equilateral triangle?

16. Fill in the remaining column in the *Polygon Angles Data Table*.

Student Guide - page 199

---

10. See Figure 22 in Lesson Guide 3 for a completed data table.*

11. *N*

12. $N - 2$

13. $180 \times (N - 2)$*

14. **A.** 360°
    B. 90° (360° ÷ 4 = 90°)

15. 60°

16. See Figure 22 in Lesson Guide 3 for a completed data table.*

Student Guide (p. 200)

Homework

Use your completed *Polygon Angles Data Table* to help you complete these problems.

1. Three of the angles of a quadrilateral have angle measures of 59°, 136°, and 89°. What is the measure of the remaining angle?

2. Four of the angles of a pentagon have angle measures of 74°, 120°, 138°, and 143°. What is the measure of the remaining angle?

3. Two angles of a hexagon have equal measure. The other angles have measures of 83°, 97°, 126°, and 98°. How many degrees are each of the two remaining angles?

4. **A.** Draw an octagon.
   B. Find two different ways of triangulating the octagon. Use different colored pencils or pens to help you.
   C. How many triangles are formed when an octagon is triangulated?
   D. What is the sum of the angles of an octagon?

What do you call a lost parrot?

A "polygon."

5. **A.** What is the sum of the angles in degrees of a regular 15-gon (a polygon with 15 sides)?
   B. What is the measure of one angle of a regular 15-gon?

6. **A.** What is the sum of the angles in degrees of a regular 20-gon?
   B. What is the measure of one angle of a regular 20-gon?

Student Guide - page 200

Homework

1. 76°

2. 65°

3. 158°

4. **A.–B.** Octagons will vary.

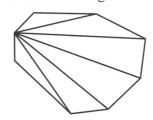 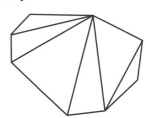

   C. 6 triangles
   D. 1080°

5. **A.** 2340°
   B. 156°

6. **A.** 3240°
   B. 162°

---

*Answers and/or discussion are included in the Lesson Guide.

Discovery Assignment Book (p. 82)

Home Practice*

Part 4. Practicing Multiplication and Division

A. 4856

B. 1566

C. 145

D. 46 R6

E. 23,155

F. 153 R3

G. 2312

H. 82 R3

I. 413

Name _____ Date _____

PART 3 **Angles and Triangles**

You will need a protractor to complete this section. Use the straight edge on your protractor to draw the angles and triangle in Questions 1, 2, and 4.

1. On a separate sheet of paper, draw an angle that is greater than 90°. Name the angle YTV. Then measure the angle to the nearest degree.

2. On a separate sheet of paper, draw an angle that is less than 45°. Name the angle RGM. Then measure the angle to the nearest degree.

3. If triangle ADK has two angles that are 40° each, what is the measure of the third angle? How do you know?

4. Can a triangle have two 70° angles and one that measures 50°? How do you know?

5. One angle in triangle QFP is a right angle. A second angle is 27°. What is the measure of the third angle? How do you know?

6. One angle in a triangle measures 32°. Another angle is twice as large. What is the measure of the third angle? How do you know?

PART 4 **Practicing Multiplication and Division**

Use paper and pencil to solve the following problems. Estimate to be sure your answers are reasonable. Use a separate sheet of paper to show your work.

A. $607 \times 8 =$ _____   B. $174 \times 9 =$ _____   C. $435 \div 3 =$ _____

D. $420 \div 9 =$ _____   E. $4631 \times 5 =$ _____   F. $768 \div 5 =$ _____

G. $68 \times 34 =$ _____   H. $577 \div 7 =$ _____   I. $1652 \div 4 =$ _____

82   DAB • Grade 5 • Unit 6   GEOMETRY

Discovery Assignment Book - page 82

Discovery Assignment Book (p. 91)

Polygon Angles Data Table

See Figure 22 in Lesson Guide 3 for a completed data table.*

Name _____ Date _____

Polygon Angles Data Table

Fill in the rows for the triangle, quadrilateral, and pentagon. Leave the last column blank. Then complete the table through the dodecagon (12-sided polygon). Your class will discuss the entries for the final column and last row.

Polygon	Number of Sides	Number of Angles	Number of Triangles	Sum of Angles (degrees)	Measure of One Angle of a Regular Polygon (degrees)
triangle					
quadrilateral					
pentagon					
hexagon					
septagon					
octagon					
nonagon					
decagon					
11-gon					
dodecagon					
N-gon					

Polygon Angles   DAB • Grade 5 • Unit 6 • Lesson 3   91

Discovery Assignment Book - page 91

*Answers for all the Home Practice in the *Discovery Assignment Book* are at the end of the unit.

Lesson
4
Congruent Shapes

Lesson Overview

Estimated Class Sessions

1

Students explore properties of triangles and discuss congruence of figures.

Key Content

- Investigating properties of triangles.
- Exploring congruence and similarity.
- Making and testing conjectures about geometric properties.

Key Vocabulary

- congruent
- similar

Math Facts

Complete DPP item K for this lesson.

Homework

1. Assign the Homework section in the *Student Guide.*
2. Assign Part 6 of the Home Practice.

Assessment

1. Use DPP Task L Drawing Shapes as a quiz.
2. Use the *Observational Assessment Record* to document students' abilities to identify congruent and similar shapes.

Materials List

Supplies and Copies

Student	Teacher
Supplies for Each Student • scissors • centimeter ruler • protractor **Supplies for Each Student Group** • 10 straws plus extras • 4 chenille sticks plus extras	**Supplies** • 10 straws • 4 chenille sticks cut into approximately 5-cm lengths
Copies	**Copies/Transparencies** • 1 transparency of *Congruent Shapes Examples* (*Unit Resource Guide* Page 78) • 1 transparency of *A Triangle* (*Unit Resource Guide* Page 79) • 1 transparency of *Congruent Shapes,* optional (*Student Guide* Pages 201–202)

All blackline masters including assessment, transparency, and DPP masters are also on the Teacher Resource CD.

Student Books
Congruent Shapes (*Student Guide* Pages 201–204)

Daily Practice and Problems and Home Practice
DPP items K–L (*Unit Resource Guide* Pages 21–22)
Home Practice Part 6 (*Discovery Assignment Book* Page 83)

Note: Classrooms whose pacing differs significantly from the suggested pacing of the units should use the Math Facts Calendar in Section 4 of the *Facts Resource Guide* to ensure students receive the complete math facts program.

Assessment Tools
Observational Assessment Record (*Unit Resource Guide* Pages 11–12)

Daily Practice and Problems

Suggestions for using the DPPs are on page 76.

K. Bit: Cristina's News Station
(URG p. 21)

Cristina's News Station has 7 programs every half hour: the international news, local news, weather, traffic, advertising, Joke of the Day, and Today's Music Single. If each program is the same length, approximately how many minutes long is each program?

L. Task: Drawing Shapes (URG p. 22)

1. Draw triangle JKL using these directions:
   A. Make ∠K measure 70°.
   B. Make $\overline{JK}$ measure 3 cm.
   C. Make $\overline{JK}$ measure 5 cm.

2. Draw triangle PQR using these directions:
   A. Make ∠Q measure 70°.
   B. Make $\overline{PQ}$ twice the length of $\overline{JK}$.
   C. Make $\overline{QR}$ twice the length of $\overline{KL}$.

3. A. Are your two shapes congruent?
   B. Are they similar?
   C. Measure ∠J and ∠P. What do you find?

Part 1 Making Triangles

Ask students to cut straws into 3 lengths, each measuring a whole number of centimeters. To make working with the straw pieces easier, require that they cut pieces greater than 2 cm. For example, children might cut:

6 cm, 8 cm, and 8 cm;
or 3 cm, 4 cm, and 5 cm;
or 3 cm, 3 cm, and 10 cm.

Now ask children to connect the straw pieces using pieces of chenille stick (cut about 5 cm in length) as connectors. Many groups will be able to form triangles, but some will not because of the lengths they chose. Figure 23 illustrates such a possibility.

Figure 23: *An incomplete triangle*

Find a group whose lengths do not close to form a triangle and hold up the incomplete triangle. Ask:

- *Why do these lengths not work? How could you change the situation so you could make a triangle?*

Children will see that one or both of the sides must be made longer (or the long side made shorter). Discuss how much longer one of the shorter pieces must be to make a triangle. If you are using the 3 cm, 3 cm, and 10 cm pieces, they will note that extending one of the shorter sides to 7 cm and combining it with the other 3 cm piece gives a length equivalent to the 10 cm piece. This is a flat triangle. (Mathematicians sometimes refer to these as degenerate triangles.)

Prompt children to discover that to get a triangle, the sum of the two shorter sides must be greater than 10 cm. Ask students to generalize:

- *Can you predict whether three lengths will or will not form a triangle? Can you find a rule?*

Allow students to discuss this in groups. Eventually guide the discussion to conclude that the sum of any two sides of a triangle must be greater than the third to form a triangle.

For those groups who could not make a triangle, ask them to make one now by changing one of their pieces.

> ### TIMS Tip
>
> Before the lesson, prepare 3 lengths of straws that will not form a triangle in case no group chooses such lengths. For example, 3 cm, 3 cm, and 10 cm pieces do not form a triangle.

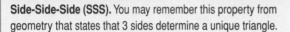
Ask students to cut three new pieces measuring the same sizes as the ones they used to make the first triangle. Tell students to make a new triangle, different from the one they made previously. Give students a chance to work on this problem. You will soon hear questions (or complaints). They may ask you what you mean by "different." Lead the class to see that triangles that can be placed one on top of the other with edges and angles fitting exactly can be considered the same. We call such triangles (and shapes in general) **congruent.** When two shapes are congruent, the corresponding (matching) sides are the same length and the corresponding angles have the same measure.

This activity shows that when three lengths make a triangle, they always make the same triangle. It is impossible to make a different triangle, using the same three lengths.

To explore congruence further, show students the top of the *Congruent Shapes Examples* transparency. Ask:

* *Do you think the two figures on the top are congruent?*

* *Do you think the two figures on the bottom are congruent?*

It is often difficult to decide congruence simply by looking. One way to decide is to measure all the sides and angles and determine whether matching sides and angles are equal. An easier way is to trace one figure on a sheet of paper (or acetate, if using the overhead) and see if one figure can be laid exactly on the other. The two figures on the top of the transparency are not congruent, but the figures on the bottom are congruent. Illustrate this to students. Talk about doing flips and turns to ascertain whether the shapes are congruent. If one of the figures on the bottom of the transparency is turned and flipped, the two figures fit exactly over one another.

Part 2 Copying Triangles

Show *A Triangle* transparency from the *Unit Resource Guide.* Ask students working in their groups to make a copy of this triangle on a sheet of paper. At first, this seems like an easy task. They soon find that it is difficult using just a ruler. Some may use straws or mark other objects with the needed lengths. Others may think of coming up and measuring an angle. Allow them to do so. Encourage different strategies and tools. Ask:

• *What information would help us perform the task more easily?*

They may suggest angle measures. At this point, label *one* of the angle measures and ask students to copy the triangle now. The angle measures are shown in Figure 24. They should find this much easier now. Ask:

• *What happens when two sides and the angle between the two sides are already drawn? What happens to the third side?* (Children might see that the third side is fixed. That is, there is no choice of length for the third side.)

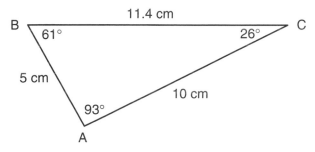

Figure 24: *The angle measures for Triangle ABC on the A Triangle Transparency Master*

Content Note

Side-Angle-Side. In later work in geometry, students will learn that fixing two sides and the included angle determines a unique triangle. This is known as the SAS (side-angle-side) property.

Discuss the introduction on the *Congruent Shapes* Activity Pages in the *Student Guide*. Examples of congruent shapes and similar shapes are provided. **Similar** shapes have the same shape, but not necessarily the same size. Assign students to do Explore *Questions 1–4* in pairs. In *Question 1*, all triangles will be congruent if constructed accurately. Once the two sides (AB and AC) and the included angle (∠A) are drawn, the third side is determined. In *Questions 2–3*, not enough information is given to ensure that everyone will draw congruent shapes. The quadrilaterals students draw in *Question 4* should all be similar. The three sides and the two included angles determine the length of the fourth side and the two remaining angles.

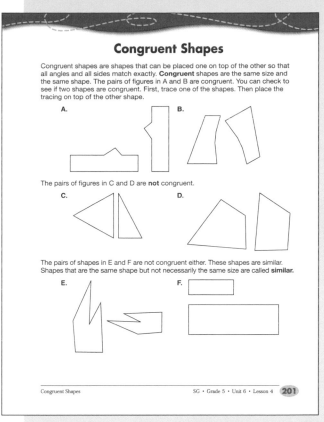

Student Guide - page 201

Student Guide - page 202 (Answers on p. 80)

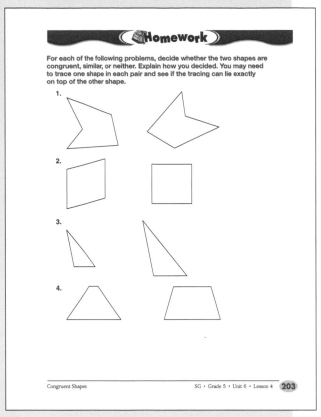
DPP item K reviews a division fact in the context of time.

Homework and Practice

- The *Congruent Shapes* Activity Pages in the *Student Guide* provide homework **Questions 1–8.**

- Assign Part 6 of the Home Practice that includes fraction problems. Make *Centimeter Dot Paper* available.

Answers for Part 6 of the Home Practice are in the Answer Key at the end of this lesson and at the end of this unit.

Assessment

- Use DPP Task L as a quiz.

- Use the *Observational Assessment Record* to document students' abilities to identify congruent and similar shapes.

Software Connection

The Explore Transformation feature of *Tessellation Exploration* allows students to further study congruency through investigations of flips, turns, and slides of geometric figures.

---

5. Draw triangle PQR. Side PQ = 6 cm, the measure of ∠P is 90°, side PR = 4 cm. Do you think everyone will draw the same triangle? Why or why not?

6. Draw rectangle WXYZ. Make Side XY = 5 cm. Make Side YZ = 7 cm. Do you think everyone will draw the same rectangle? Why or why not?

7. Draw triangle STU. Make Sides ST and TU the same length. Make ∠T = 75°. Do you think everyone will draw the same triangle? Why or why not?

8. Draw quadrilateral ABCD. Make Angles B and C both measure 110°. Side BC is 6 cm. Do you think everyone will draw the same quadrilateral? Why or why not?

Student Guide - page 204 *(Answers on p. 81)*

Name _____   Date _____

PART 5 **Slab-Maker Problems**
Draw these shapes and answer the questions on a separate sheet of paper. You will need a centimeter ruler and a protractor.

1. Draw triangle DEF. The length of side EF is 5 cm. Angle F is a right angle. The length of DF is 12 cm. What is the length of side DE?

2. Draw rectangle GHIJ. The length of GH is 8 cm. The length of HI is half the length of GH. What is the area of this rectangle?

3. Draw quadrilateral QRST. The length of ST is 6 cm. Angles S and T are both 60°. The lengths of sides RS and QT are 2 cm. Which two line segments are parallel?

4. Draw a pentagon with two right angles. Have one side measure 4 cm and one side measure 5 cm. Do you think everyone will draw congruent pentagons? How do you know?

PART 6 **Fractions**

1. Solve the following addition and subtraction problems.

   A. $\frac{1}{2} + \frac{5}{8} =$ _____   B. $\frac{2}{3} + \frac{1}{12} =$ _____

   C. $\frac{7}{12} - \frac{1}{2} =$ _____   D. $\frac{3}{5} - \frac{3}{10} =$ _____

2. Draw pictures to help you answer these questions. You may use dot paper to help you.

   A. One furlong is $\frac{1}{8}$ mile. How many furlongs equal one mile?

   B. A tablespoon is $\frac{1}{16}$ of a cup. How many tablespoons equal one cup?

   C. One foot is $\frac{1}{3}$ of a yard. How many feet equal one yard?

   D. Five minutes is $\frac{1}{12}$ of an hour. How many minutes equal $\frac{3}{12}$ of an hour?

   E. Gold that is pure is called 24 karat gold. If 1 out of 24 parts is pure, it is 1 karat gold. Gold that is 10 karat is $\frac{10}{24}$ or $\frac{5}{12}$ pure. Is 14 karat gold more or less than $\frac{1}{2}$ pure gold?

GEOMETRY   DAB • Grade 5 • Unit 6   **83**

Discovery Assignment Book - page 83 *(Answers on p. 81)*

At a Glance

Math Facts and Daily Practice and Problems

Complete DPP items K and L for this lesson.

Part 1. Making Triangles

1. Students cut straws into three lengths and try to make a triangle using chenille sticks as connectors.
2. Students determine from their constructions that the sum of any two sides of a triangle must be greater than the third.
3. By using the same three lengths, students discover that three sides determine a unique triangle.
4. Display the *Congruent Shapes Examples* transparency. Discuss how to determine if two shapes are congruent.

Part 2. Copying Triangles

1. Display A *Triangle* transparency and ask students to copy the triangle.
2. Discuss the difficulty of copying a triangle without knowing an angle.
3. Give students one of the angle measures of the triangle and have them complete the task.
4. Students read the *Congruent Shapes* Activity Pages in the *Student Guide.*
5. Students complete *Questions 1–4* in pairs. Discuss their answers.

Homework

1. Assign the Homework section in the *Student Guide.*
2. Assign Part 6 of the Home Practice.

Assessment

1. Use DPP Task L *Drawing Shapes* as a quiz.
2. Use the *Observational Assessment Record* to document students' abilities to identify congruent and similar shapes.

Connection

Use the Explore Transformation feature in *Tessellation Exploration* to further study congruency.

Answer Key is on pages 80–81.

Notes:

Congruent Shapes Examples

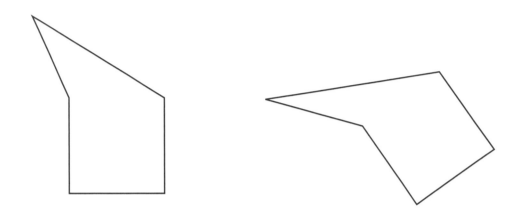

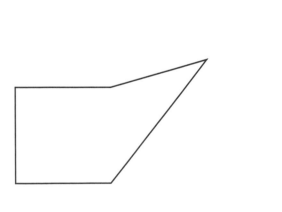
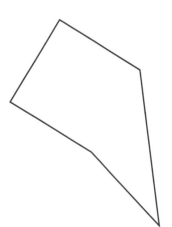

Transparency Master

A Triangle

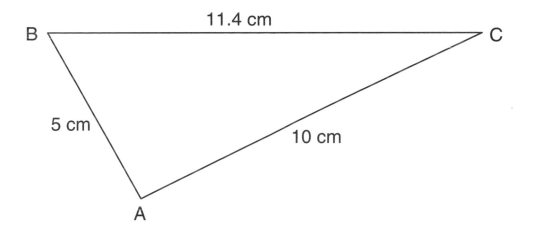

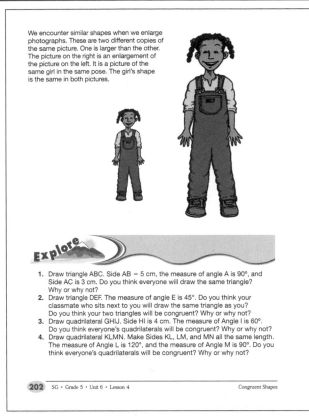

We encounter similar shapes when we enlarge photographs. These are two different copies of the same picture. One is larger than the other. The picture on the right is an enlargement of the picture on the left. It is a picture of the same girl in the same pose. The girl's shape is the same in both pictures.

Explore

1. Draw triangle ABC. Side AB = 5 cm, the measure of angle A is 90°, and Side AC is 3 cm. Do you think everyone will draw the same triangle? Why or why not?
2. Draw triangle DEF. The measure of angle E is 45°. Do you think your classmate who sits next to you will draw the same triangle as you? Do you think your two triangles will be congruent? Why or why not?
3. Draw quadrilateral GHIJ. Side HI is 4 cm. The measure of Angle I is 60°. Do you think everyone's quadrilaterals will be congruent? Why or why not?
4. Draw quadrilateral KLMN. Make Sides KL, LM, and MN all the same length. The measure of Angle L is 120°, and the measure of Angle M is 90°. Do you think everyone's quadrilaterals will be congruent? Why or why not?

202   SG • Grade 5 • Unit 6 • Lesson 4   Congruent Shapes

Student Guide - page 202

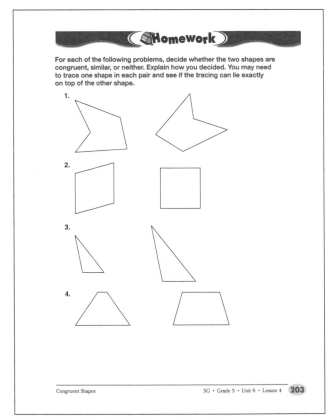

Homework

For each of the following problems, decide whether the two shapes are congruent, similar, or neither. Explain how you decided. You may need to trace one shape in each pair and see if the tracing can lie exactly on top of the other shape.

1.
2.
3.
4.

Congruent Shapes   SG • Grade 5 • Unit 6 • Lesson 4   203

Student Guide - page 203

Student Guide (pp. 202–203)

1. Yes*

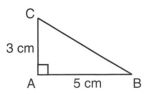

2. No, students can make sides DE and DF as long as they want.*

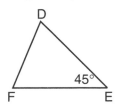

3. No, students can make sides IJ and HG as long as they want.*

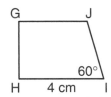

4. No, but they should be similar.*

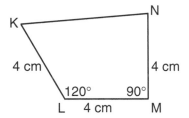

Homework

1. Congruent. Each pair of corresponding sides and angles are the same measurement.
2. Neither. The one on the right is a square (its angles are right angles and the sides are all the same length) whereas the one on the left is not.
3. Similar. They are the same shape but not the same size.
4. Neither. The corresponding sides and angles are not the same measurement. They aren't the same shape.

*Answers and/or discussion are included in the Lesson Guide.

Student Guide (p. 204)

5. Yes

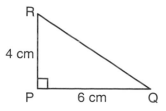

6. Yes

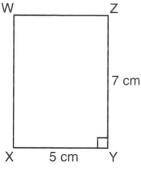

7. No, but they should be similar.

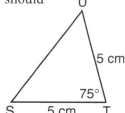

8. No, students can make sides BA and CD as long as they want.

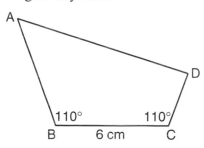

Discovery Assignment Book (p. 83)

Home Practice*

Part 6. Fractions

I. **A.** $\frac{9}{8}$ **B.** $\frac{9}{12}$ or $\frac{3}{4}$

  C. $\frac{1}{12}$ **D.** $\frac{3}{10}$

2. **A.** 8 furlongs   **B.** 16 tablespoons

  C. 3 feet   **D.** 15 minutes

  E. more

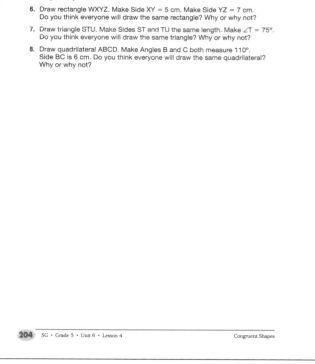

Student Guide - page 204

Discovery Assignment Book - page 83

*Answers for all the Home Practice in the *Discovery Assignment Book* are at the end of the unit.

Optional Lesson 5

Quilts and Tessellations

Lesson Overview

Estimated Class Sessions

3

Children learn about properties of polygons by investigating tessellations. They analyze quilt patterns and design their own tessellations. This activity can be completed as an art connection.

Key Content

- Investigating the properties of polygons.
- Investigating tessellations.
- Developing deductive reasoning.
- Connecting mathematics and art: tessellations

Key Vocabulary

- quilt
- tessellation

Homework

Students complete the homework questions on the *Quilts and Tessellations* Activity Pages in the *Student Guide*.

Assessment

Use homework *Questions 1–2* as an assessment.

Materials List

Supplies and Copies

Student	Teacher
Supplies for Each Student • protractor • plain unlined paper, optional **Supplies for Each Student Group** • 1 set of pattern blocks (12 green triangles, 12 orange squares, 3 yellow hexagons, 6 red trapezoids, 6 blue rhombuses, 12 tan rhombuses)	**Supplies** • overhead pattern blocks, optional • protractor
Copies • 3 copies of *Triangle Grid Paper* per student plus extras, optional (*Unit Resource Guide* Page 94)	**Copies/Transparencies** • 1 transparency of *Jacob's Ladder Quilt* (*Unit Resource Guide* Page 89) • 1 transparency of *Detail View of Jacob's Ladder Quilt* (*Unit Resource Guide* Page 90) • 1 transparency of *Four Quilt Patterns* (*Unit Resource Guide* Pages 91–92) • 1 transparency of *Regular Hexagons* (*Unit Resource Guide* Page 93)

All blackline masters including assessment, transparency, and DPP masters are also on the Teacher Resource CD.

Student Books

Quilts and Tessellations (*Student Guide* Pages 205–209)

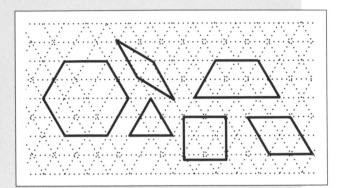

Figure 25: *Pattern block pieces on* Triangle Grid Paper

Quilts and Tessellations

Quilts are a part of our American heritage. Quilts are used as blankets, but many quilts are also works of art. Why talk about quilts in a math class? As you can see in the picture, quilts often include many interesting geometric shapes and patterns. What patterns do you see in this quilt called Jacob's Ladder?

Student Guide - page 205

Before the Activity

To enrich the activity, find books on quilts, Islamic art, or other art genres that utilize geometric patterns. Perhaps you or a colleague have a quilt at home to bring in to show the class. Also, you might be able to find a person knowledgeable about these art forms to talk to your students.

The *Triangle Grid Paper* is provided for students who find it easier to trace the pattern blocks on the grid paper than on plain paper. For this lesson, the grid paper, which consists of $\frac{1}{2}$-inch equilateral triangles, may be easier for children to use because the pattern blocks fit on the lines as in Figure 25. Note, however, that the square and the tan rhombus do not fit properly on the grid lines. Some students may want to use the grid paper while others may prefer to use plain paper. You may do part of the lesson on grid paper and then have students make their own designs on large sheets of plain paper.

Teaching the Activity

Begin class by showing the *Jacob's Ladder Quilt* transparency from the *Unit Resource Guide.* This picture is also in the *Student Guide.* Note that there are variations of this quilt and using different color combinations can change the look considerably. Also, many of the same quilt patterns have different names.

Some quilts use geometric patterns for their designs. Ask students to take a better look at the *Jacob's Ladder Quilt* and describe some of the geometric patterns they see. Show them the *Detail View of Jacob's Ladder Quilt* Transparency Master to help them see more patterns. This transparency shows the center block of the quilt.

Content Note

Quilts. A quilt is a blanket, but it can also be a work of art. American pioneers made quilts. They were often made very economically from scraps of fabric (patches) and pieces could be replaced as they became worn. Other quilts were carefully planned, with fabrics, designs, and colors chosen to be pleasing to the eye. Quilts were sewn by hand, requiring tremendous amounts of time. Sometimes women would work on a quilt together to make the work go faster. This was also a way to get together socially while still getting their work done.

There are many patterns to see in this quilt. Some of them are:

- The quilt is made up of squares and right triangles.
- The quilt is composed of nine large blocks.
- The nine large blocks are made of 4 small blocks (the detailed view), which are, in turn, divided into 4 unit squares.
- The area of two unit squares must be the same as the area of one of the large triangles since each occupies half a small block.
- All triangle blocks are positioned to get the ladder effect.

Note to students that all the pieces fit together exactly, leaving no gaps or overlaps. We know the angles of the square are 90°. Ask:

- *What are the measures of the angles of the triangle?*

Students may realize the right triangle must have acute angles measuring 45° each. Because at any point where pieces come together, the sum of the pieces must be 360°. It is easy to see that the two acute angles are the same size, thus each must be 45°. Therefore, there are no gaps and no overlaps. You do not need to discuss this with students yet. It will evolve as the lesson progresses. It is better for them to discover this for themselves.

Ask students to look at the picture of four quilt patterns (shown here in Figure 26) in the *Student Guide.* These quilt patterns were chosen because they can be made from the pattern blocks. Have students duplicate these patterns using the blocks. *(Question 1)* Make sure they extend the patterns. Students will in effect be making quilts as shown in Figure 27. Assign groups to do a specific pattern or allow them to choose.

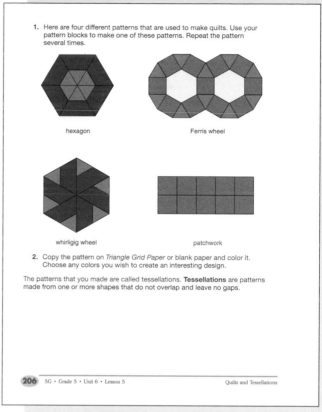

1. Here are four different patterns that are used to make quilts. Use your pattern blocks to make one of these patterns. Repeat the pattern several times.

hexagon   Ferris wheel

whirligig wheel   patchwork

2. Copy the pattern on *Triangle Grid Paper* or blank paper and color it. Choose any colors you wish to create an interesting design.

The patterns that you made are called tessellations. **Tessellations** are patterns made from one or more shapes that do not overlap and leave no gaps.

Student Guide - page 206 (Answers on p. 95)

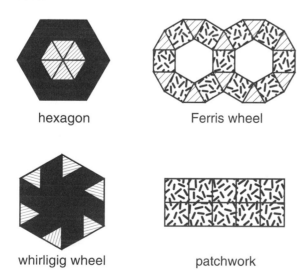

hexagon   Ferris wheel

whirligig wheel   patchwork

Figure 26: *Four quilt patterns*

Figure 27: *Extended pattern for the Ferris wheel*

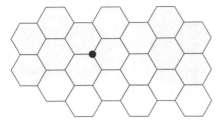

3. A large dot has been placed where three hexagons come together. We call this a **vertex** of the tessellation. Why do the three hexagons fit exactly, leaving no gaps? (*Hint:* Think about the angles at the vertex.)

4. **A.** Copy the hexagon tessellation with your pattern blocks. Then sketch part of it on *Triangle Grid Paper* or blank paper.
   B. Mark another vertex. Are the angles at your new vertex the same as those in the drawing above?
   C. Find the sum of the angles at the new vertex.

5. **A.** Look at the close-up of the Ferris wheel pattern. Notice a large dot has been placed where a hexagon, square, triangle, and square come together. Why do the pieces fit together exactly? (*Hint:* Think about the angles at the vertex.)

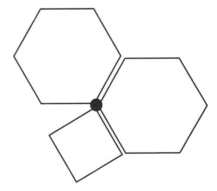

   B. Copy the Ferris wheel pattern with your pattern blocks. Then sketch it.

Quilts and Tessellations   SG • Grade 5 • Unit 6 • Lesson 5   **207**

***Student Guide* - page 207 (Answers on p. 95)**

For **Question 2,** students draw the patterns on paper. (You may wish to use the *Triangle Grid Paper* instead of plain paper.) Have them choose colors for each different shape (not necessarily the pattern block colors) to decorate their designs.

Explain to students that all the patterns they made and looked at are called tessellations. **Tessellations** are patterns made up of one or more shapes that completely cover a surface without any gaps or overlaps.

Questions 3–4 ask students to look at the tessellation of regular hexagons. Show the *Regular Hexagons* transparency from the *Unit Resource Guide* on the overhead projector. Use the following prompts to encourage small group discussion:

- *Why do the three hexagons fit together exactly, leaving no gaps?*

If students are having difficulties, use the pattern blocks to make the pattern but substitute a square for one of the hexagons, as in Figure 28.

- *Why don't the two hexagons and the square fit exactly?*

Eventually, students will recall their work with angle measures. They may wish to look at the Polygons Data Table in Lesson 3. They will see that the three hexagons fit exactly because each angle is 120 degrees. Remind them the hexagon is a regular hexagon. The three together form 360 degrees—in other words, a complete circle. They leave no gaps and do not overlap. Use the *Regular Hexagons* Transparency Master to show this.

Figure 28: *Two hexagons and a square*

Content Note

Tessellating Regular Polygons. The only regular polygons that tessellate are the triangle, square, and hexagon.

Question 5 asks students to look at the pattern in the Ferris wheel quilt shown in Figure 26 and on the *Four Quilt Patterns* Transparency Masters. Here, students must realize that the angles of a hexagon, square, triangle, and another square come together, giving a total of 120 + 90 + 60 + 90 = 360 degrees.

Questions 6–7 ask students to make their own tessellation with the pattern blocks and draw it on paper. Make sure their patterns repeat. Then students need to find the sum of the angles at a vertex in their tessellation.

Journal Prompt

Can regular triangles be laid so there are no gaps? In other words, do regular triangles (equilateral triangles) tessellate? Explain why.

Homework and Practice

Homework is provided in the *Quilts and Tessellations* Activity Pages in the *Student Guide*.

Assessment

You can use Homework **Questions 1–2** on the *Quilts and Tessellations* Activity Pages to assess students' understanding of tessellations.

Extension

- Geometry in art provides a wealth of possible extensions. You may explore a famous artist such as M.C. Escher. Exploring Islamic art or other cultural art is another interesting extension.

- Children can explore quilts more thoroughly. A bulletin board of colored tessellations or quilts makes a wonderful display to illustrate connections between mathematics and art.

Literature Connections

- Friedman, Aileen. *A Cloak for the Dreamer.* Scholastic, 1994.

- Hopkinson, Deborah. *Sweet Clara and the Freedom Quilt.* Paintings by James Ransome. Alfred A. Knopf, New York, 1993.

- Kinsey-Warnock, Natalie. *The Canada Geese Quilt.* Illustrated by Leslie W. Bowman. Cobblehill Books/Dutton, New York, 1989.

- Paul, Ann Whitford. *The Seasons Sewn: A Year in Patchwork.* Harcourt Brace & Co., New York, 1996.

- ——. *Eight Hands Round A Patchwork Alphabet.* Illustrated by Jeanette Winter. Harper Collins, New York, 1991.

C. Draw another vertex. Are the angles at your new vertex the same as those in the drawing?
D. Find the sum of the angles at the new vertex.
E. Why do the angles at each vertex fit together and leave no gaps?

6. Use pattern blocks to make your own tessellation. Record it on the grid paper. Color it to make an interesting design.

7. A. Draw a vertex on your tessellation.
B. Find the sum of the angles at your vertex.

Homework

1. Look at the close-up of the whirligig wheel. Notice the large dot where two triangles and two rhombuses come together. Why do the pieces fit together exactly?

2. Can a tessellation be made using only regular pentagons? Why or why not? A regular pentagon is pictured here. You may wish to trace it.

Student Guide - page 208 (Answers on p. 96)

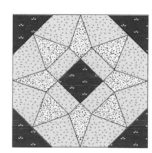

3. Quilts can contain many more geometric shapes than those seen in pattern blocks. The quilt design shown above is used to make the quilt called North Carolina Star. Describe the geometric shapes you see.

Student Guide - page 209 (Answers on p. 96)

At a Glance

Teaching the Activity

1. Show the class the *Jacob's Ladder Quilt* transparency and discuss the geometry of the quilt pattern. The quilt is on the first *Quilts and Tessellations* Activity Page in the *Student Guide.*

2. Students use pattern blocks to make quilt patterns shown in the *Student Guide. (Question 1)*

3. Students trace and color their quilt patterns on paper. *(Question 2)*

4. Students examine which patterns tessellate and why. *(Questions 3–5)*

5. Students design their own tessellations. *(Questions 6–7)*

Homework

Students complete the homework questions on the *Quilts and Tessellations* Activity Pages in the *Student Guide.*

Assessment

Use homework *Questions 1–2* as an assessment.

Extension

1. Explore famous geometric artists such as M.C. Escher.

2. Make a bulletin board of quilts or tessellations.

Connection

Read and explore books such as *A Cloak for the Dreamer, Sweet Clara and the Freedom Quilt*, or *The Canada Geese Quilt.*

Answer Key is on pages 95–96.

Notes:

Jacob's Ladder Quilt

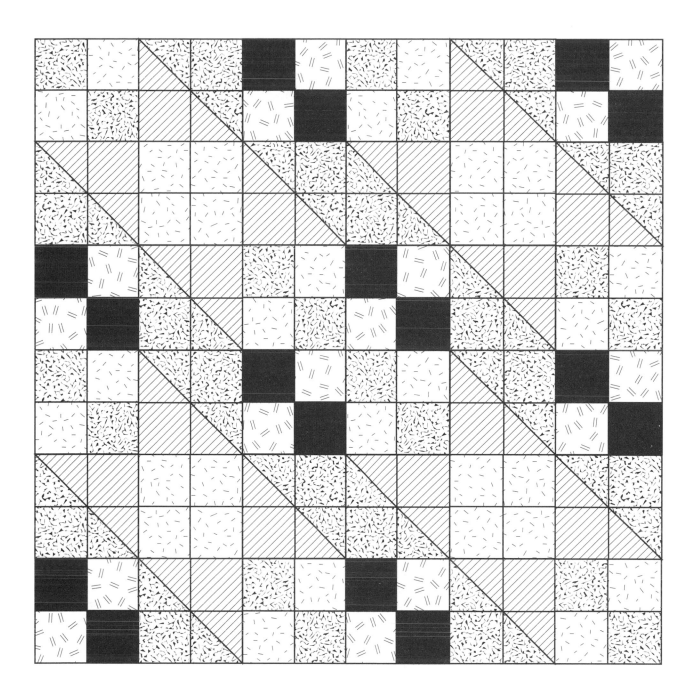

Detail View of
Jacob's Ladder Quilt

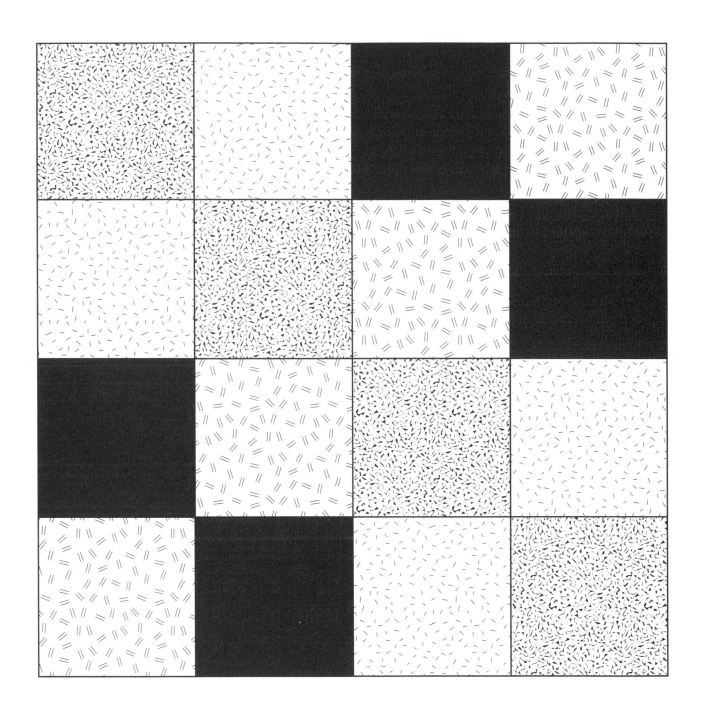

Transparency Master

Four Quilt Patterns

patchwork

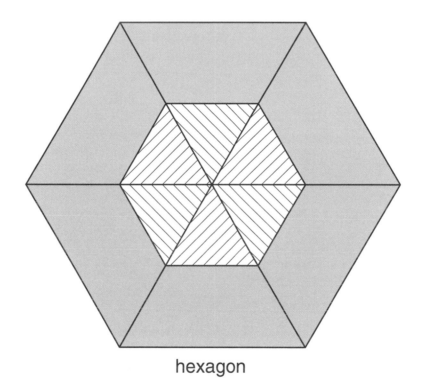

hexagon

Four Quilt Patterns

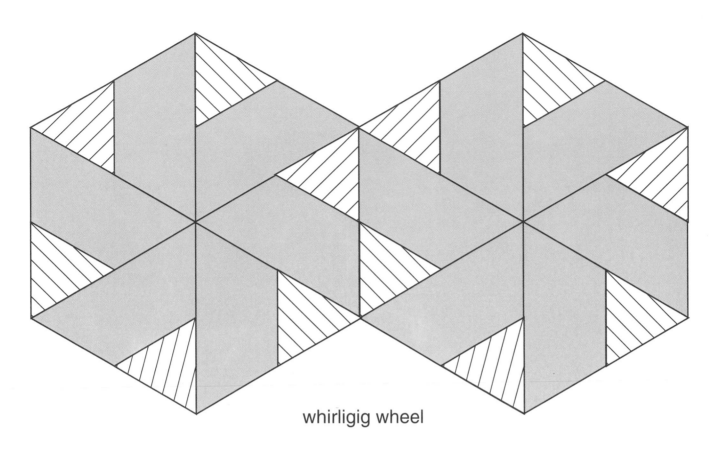

whirligig wheel

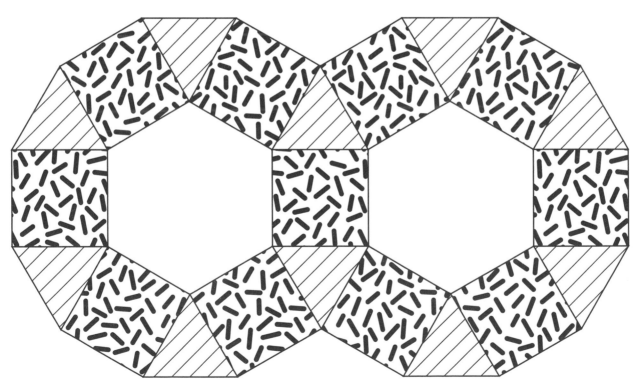

Ferris wheel

Transparency Master

Regular Hexagons

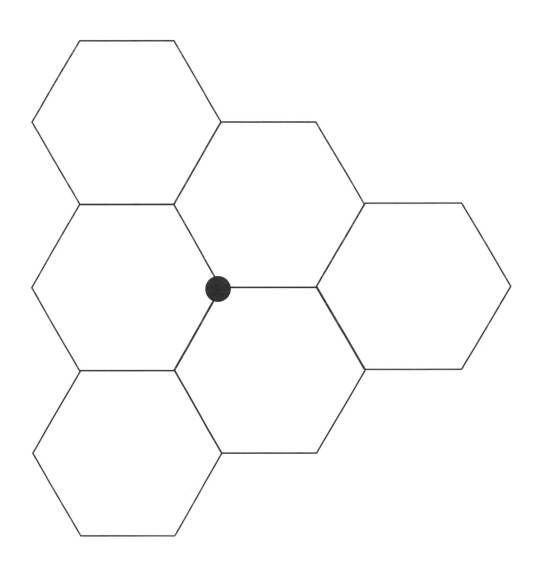

Triangle Grid Paper

Student Guide (p. 206)

1.–2. Designs will vary.

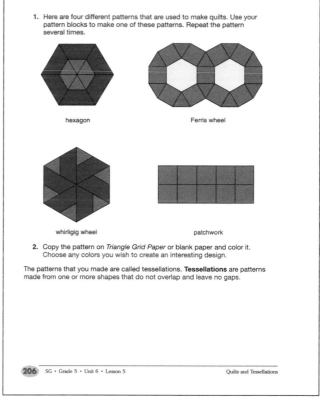

Student Guide - page 206

Student Guide (p. 207)

3. Each of the three angles coming together at the vertex are 120°; 120° × 3 = 360° or a complete circle.*

4. A.–B. Yes

   C. 360°

5. A. The triangle's angle is 60°. Two right angles are each 90°. The hexagon's angle is 120°; 60° + 90° + 90° + 120° = 360°.*

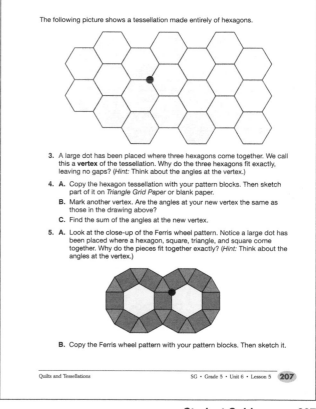

Student Guide - page 207

*Answers and/or discussion are included in the Lesson Guide.

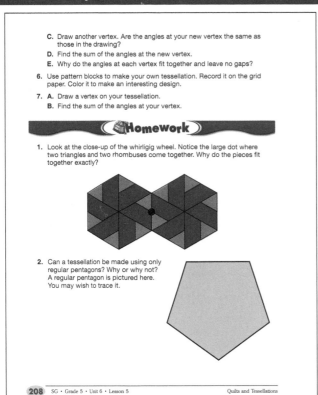

Student Guide - page 208

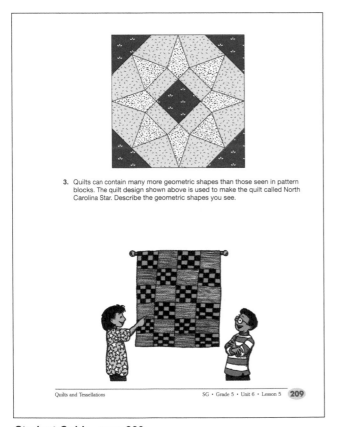

Student Guide - page 209

Student Guide (p. 208)

B.–C. Yes

D. 360°

E. The triangle's angle is 60°. Two right angles are each 90°. The hexagon's angle is 120°; 60° + 90° + 90° + 120° = 360°.

6. Answers will vary.

7. A. Answers will vary.

B. 360°

Homework

1. Each of the two blue rhombus angles is 120°. Each of the two green triangle angles is 60°; 120° + 120° + 60° + 60° = 360°.

2. No. Each angle in a regular pentagon is 108°; 108° does not divide into 360 evenly.

Student Guide (p. 209)

3. Descriptions will vary. Some shapes in the design are: rectangles, triangles, a square, and a kite.

Classifying Shapes

Lesson Overview

Estimated Class Sessions 2-3

Students explore ways to classify two-dimensional geometric figures. Students see how the mathematical classification of shapes has similarities to the classification of living things. They informally explore writing a definition for a class of geometric objects. In the context of designing a "shapes zoo," they take a collection of polygons, divide them into categories and further divide some of the categories into subcategories.

Key Content

- Describing and classifying two-dimensional shapes.
- Using mathematical definitions.
- Connecting mathematics and science: classifying animals.

Key Vocabulary

- convex
- mammal
- obtuse triangle
- parallelogram
- pentagon
- polygon
- quadrilateral
- rectangle
- rhombus
- square
- vertebrate

Math Facts

Complete DPP items O–P for this lesson.

Homework

1. Assign the Homework section in the *Student Guide* before Part 2.
2. Assign Part 7 of the Home Practice.

Assessment

You can use The Flatville Zoo section in the *Student Guide* as an assessment.

Materials List

Supplies and Copies

Student	Teacher
Supplies for Each Student • large art paper • glue • scissors	**Supplies** • dictionary
Copies	**Copies/Transparencies** • 1 transparency of *Classifying Shapes,* optional (*Student Guide* Pages 210 & 212)

All blackline masters including assessment, transparency, and DPP masters are also on the Teacher Resource CD.

Student Books

Classifying Shapes (*Student Guide* Pages 210–217)
Shapes Zoo Pieces (*Discovery Assignment Book* Page 93)

Daily Practice and Problems and Home Practice

DPP items M–P (*Unit Resource Guide* Pages 23–25)
Home Practice Part 7 (*Discovery Assignment Book* Page 84)

Note: Classrooms whose pacing differs significantly from the suggested pacing of the units should use the Math Facts Calendar in Section 4 of the *Facts Resource Guide* to ensure students receive the complete math facts program.

Daily Practice and Problems

Suggestions for using the DPPs are on pages 105–106.

M. Bit: What's Your Angle?
(URG p. 23)

Find the missing angle measurements.

1.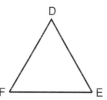

2. ∠D, ∠E, and ∠F have the same measurement.

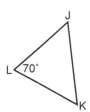

3.

4. ∠J and ∠K have the same measurement.

O. Bit: Multiplying and Dividing
with Zeros (URG p. 24)

A. 80 × 400 =

B. 2800 ÷ 70 =

C. 7 × 80,000 =

D. 700 × 6000 =

E. 4800 ÷ 600 =

F. 240 ÷ 4 =

P. Challenge: Number
Sentences with 4, 6, 7, and 8 (URG p. 25)

Use each number once in any order with any operation sign (−, +, ×, ÷) to write number sentences. You can also use parentheses. Use these numbers: 4, 6, 7, 8.

(Remember, you must use each number once, but only once.)

A. _____ = 1

B. _____ = 10

C. _____ = 20

D. _____ = 200

N. Task: Brandon the
Babysitter (URG p. 24)

1. If Brandon earns $9 for 2 hours of babysitting, what is his hourly rate?

2. A. If Brandon needs $68.25 to buy a bike, how many hours will he need to babysit?

   B. Every school day this month Brandon walks his neighbor, a second grader, home from school. He babysits her from 3 to 5:30. How many days will it take Brandon to earn the money for the bike?

3. In the summer two families used Brandon as their babysitter. He worked 8 hours a week for each family. How much did he earn in one month? (Assume there are 4 weeks in 1 month.)

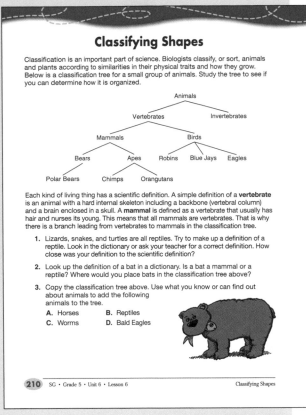

Classifying Shapes

Classification is an important part of science. Biologists classify, or sort, animals and plants according to similarities in their physical traits and how they grow. Below is a classification tree for a small group of animals. Study the tree to see if you can determine how it is organized.

Animals
— Vertebrates — Invertebrates
— Mammals — Birds
Bears — Apes — Robins — Blue Jays — Eagles
Polar Bears — Chimps — Orangutans

Each kind of living thing has a scientific definition. A simple definition of a **vertebrate** is an animal with a hard internal skeleton including a backbone (vertebral column) and a brain enclosed in a skull. A **mammal** is defined as a vertebrate that usually has hair and nurses its young. This means that all mammals are vertebrates. That is why there is a branch leading from vertebrates to mammals in the classification tree.

1. Lizards, snakes, and turtles are all reptiles. Try to make up a definition of a reptile. Look in the dictionary or ask your teacher for a correct definition. How close was your definition to the scientific definition?

2. Look up the definition of a bat in a dictionary. Is a bat a mammal or a reptile? Where would you place bats in the classification tree above?

3. Copy the classification tree above. Use what you know or can find out about animals to add the following animals to the tree.
   A. Horses   B. Reptiles
   C. Worms   D. Bald Eagles

210   SG • Grade 5 • Unit 6 • Lesson 6   Classifying Shapes

Student Guide - page 210 (Answers on p. 108)

Part 1 **Classification**

There are many ways to classify animals. The system that scientists use (including categories such as phylum, genus, and species) is based on the structure of an animal's body. This system also says something about how closely related different types of animals are. Of course, there are other ways of classifying animals.

The *Classifying Shapes* Activity Pages in the *Student Guide* include a diagram of the "classification tree" of some animals. Have students study the diagram. Ask:

* *What can you say about the animal classifications as you move down the tree?*

We hope they note that the lower you go in the tree, the narrower is the definition of that kind of animal. For example, apes and bears are both kinds of mammals, so there are branches leading from mammals to bears and apes.

Questions 1–3 ask students to add other kinds of animals to the tree. They can work in groups to copy the chart on large art paper and then add the desired types of animals. *Question 3* asks them to add horses, worms, reptiles, and bald eagles. Students probably have the knowledge needed for this, but they can always use a dictionary or other resources, such as an encyclopedia on a CD-ROM.

For example, they need to know that worms do not have backbones. After adding these types of animals, the tree should look like Figure 29.

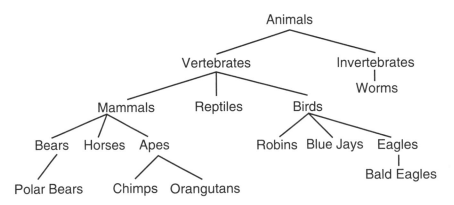

Figure 29: *Classification tree*

Classification in Geometry. Students work with a classification tree in *Questions 4–7. Question 4B* asks if every square is a rectangle. For many students, "rectangle" means "nonsquare rectangle." Let students discuss this issue. Point out that in everyday language, people may interpret "rectangle" to mean "nonsquare rectangle." But the mathematical definition of **rectangle** is a quadrilateral with four right angles. Since a square has four right angles, it must be a rectangle. A square cannot be a pentagon *(Question 4C),* since a pentagon has five sides, not four.

TIMS Tip

Students should work together to answer the questions. Encourage them to review the information in previous lessons and use resources such as dictionaries.

Question 7 asks if a quadrilateral can be both a rectangle and a rhombus. One reason for asking this question is to show that we cannot fit all geometric definitions into a tree. Since a rectangle is a quadrilateral with four right angles, and a **rhombus** is a quadrilateral with four equal sides, a shape that is both a rhombus and a rectangle is a square. Squares are branches for both rectangles and rhombuses.

Classification in Geometry
Classification is also a part of geometry. Sorting shapes into categories based upon similarities and differences helps us to understand and talk about them.

Shapes with straight sides
↓
Polygons
↙ ↘
Quadrilaterals   Triangles
↓   ↓
Rectangles   Right Triangles

4. A definition of a **rectangle** is a quadrilateral with four right angles. A definition of a **square** is a quadrilateral with four equal sides and four right angles.
   A. Is every square a quadrilateral? Why?
   B. Is every square a rectangle? Why?
   C. Can a square be a pentagon? Why?

5. Give a definition of a right triangle.

6. Copy the classification tree above. Add these shapes to the classification tree: square, pentagon, obtuse triangle.

7. A **rhombus** is a quadrilateral that has four equal sides. Can a quadrilateral be both a rhombus and a rectangle? Does this kind of shape have a name?

Classifying Shapes   SG • Grade 5 • Unit 6 • Lesson 6   **211**

Student Guide - page 211 (Answers on p. 108)

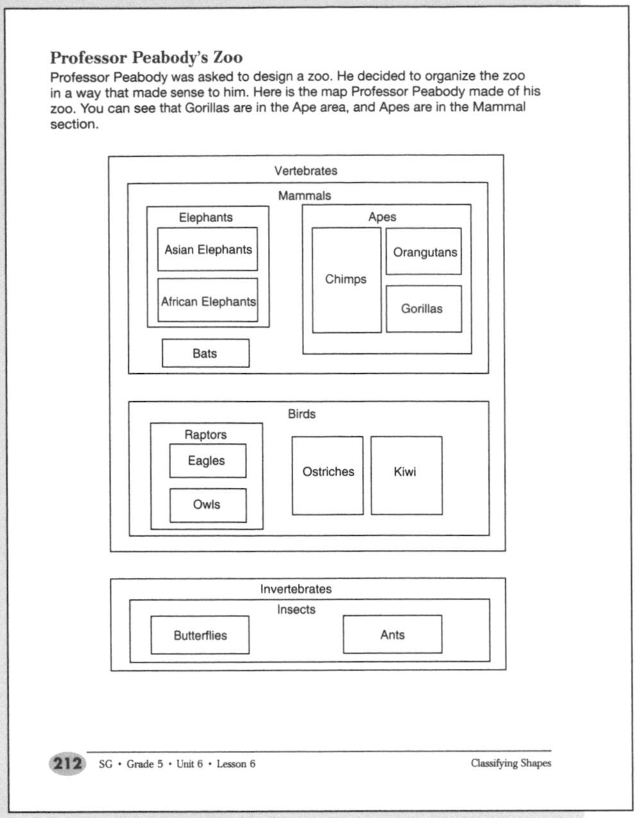

Professor Peabody's Zoo

Professor Peabody was asked to design a zoo. He decided to organize the zoo in a way that made sense to him. Here is the map Professor Peabody made of his zoo. You can see that Gorillas are in the Ape area, and Apes are in the Mammal section.

Vertebrates
Mammals
Elephants
Asian Elephants
African Elephants
Bats
Apes
Chimps
Orangutans
Gorillas
Birds
Raptors
Eagles
Owls
Ostriches
Kiwi
Invertebrates
Insects
Butterflies
Ants

212 SG • Grade 5 • Unit 6 • Lesson 6 Classifying Shapes

Student Guide* - page 212 *(Answers on p. 109)

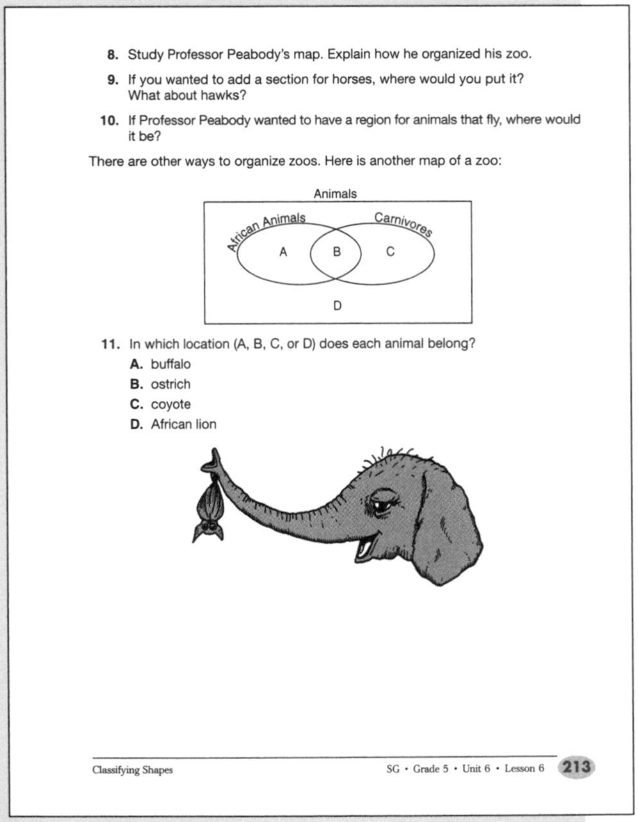

8. Study Professor Peabody's map. Explain how he organized his zoo.
9. If you wanted to add a section for horses, where would you put it? What about hawks?
10. If Professor Peabody wanted to have a region for animals that fly, where would it be?

There are other ways to organize zoos. Here is another map of a zoo:

Animals
African Animals
Carnivores
A
B
C
D

11. In which location (A, B, C, or D) does each animal belong?
    - **A.** buffalo
    - **B.** ostrich
    - **C.** coyote
    - **D.** African lion

Classifying Shapes SG • Grade 5 • Unit 6 • Lesson 6 213

Student Guide* - page 213 *(Answers on p. 109)

Some students may find this difficult to understand, perhaps because many pictures they have seen that were labeled "rhombus" did not have right angles.

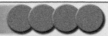

Content Note

Hierarchical Classification. The system biologists use to classify organisms is a special type, called hierarchical. In this hierarchical system, organisms are subdivided into increasingly smaller categories. Because of the subdividing, or branching, of the organisms into smaller categories, the graphical representation of this resembles, and is called, a tree. However, there are animal categories that don't fit into this system. For example, "animals that live underwater" doesn't fit because most fish and some mammals (whales, etc.) live underwater. That doesn't mean we can't talk about animals that live underwater, just that this category doesn't fit into the usual classification system. This is because the classifications are not mutually exclusive. Similarly, you can't fit all mathematical types into a tree. For example, squares are rectangles and also rhombuses. Rectangles and rhombuses are not mutually exclusive.

Professor Peabody's Zoo. In this section of the *Student Guide,* we use a different analogy for classification—the zoo. Have students look at the map of the Flatville Zoo in the *Student Guide* (or show it on an overhead). Let them discuss whether Professor Peabody's organization makes sense and where they would put other animals ***(Questions 8–10).*** In ***Question 11*** we see a zoo with two sections that overlap. This way of showing two overlapping categories is called a Venn diagram.

Assign ***Questions 1–4*** in the Homework section and discuss students' definitions of parallelogram and convex before beginning Part 2. Definitions will vary. Students should note that parallelograms have four sides and two pairs of parallel sides. The notion of convex may be easier to identify than it is to describe precisely. Students might say the polygons that are not convex "go in," while the convex ones are "rounder." A precise definition of a **convex** shape is that for any two points in the shape, the line segment between the points is also inside the shape. See Figure 30.

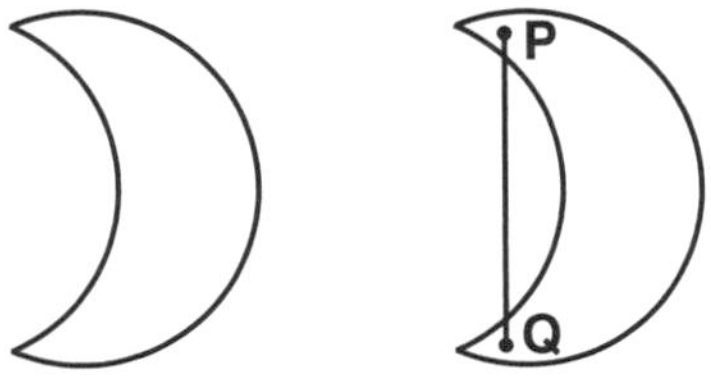

P
Q

Figure 30: *This shape is* not *convex since the line segment from P to Q is not inside the shape.*

Part 2 The Flatville Zoo

The *Student Guide* describes Professor Peabody's dream about Flatville, where all the animals are polygons. To decide how to organize the Flatville Zoo, students must decide on ways to classify the shapes (creatures in Flatville). The *Shapes Zoo Pieces* Activity Page in the *Discovery Assignment Book* can be cut into pieces containing the individual shapes. Students then sort and classify the shapes, design a Flatville Zoo on a sheet of paper, and finally put each shape in the proper place. For a more structured activity, provide them with a Flatville Zoo map based on Figure 32 and have each group place the shapes in the proper location. To ensure enough space for all the shapes, enlarge Figure 32 on a bulletin board or sheet of butcher block paper.

Our goal is for students to focus on the attributes of the polygons. Some attributes that can be used to classify shapes are:

*   number of sides,
*   length of sides,
*   angle measure,
*   symmetry, and
*   "parallelness" of sides.

Students will have an easier time categorizing the shapes than describing what the categories are. For example, they will probably put all the rectangles together and will realize that all the rectangles are quadrilaterals. However, they may not realize that every rectangle is a parallelogram. (A rectangle is a parallelogram because the opposite sides of a rectangle are parallel.) It is important to let students come up with their own categories. These categories may not have mathematical names. That's fine. If they like, they can make up a name for the category. For example, there is no common mathematical name for quadrilaterals with two pairs of equal, adjacent sides. One popular name for this type of shape is "kite" (see Figure 31). If students invent a name for a category that has a common mathematical name, you will want to tell them the mathematical name. But it is all right if they use their own invented name as well as the "official" mathematical name.

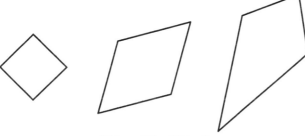

Figure 31: *"Kites"*

The Flatville Zoo

Professor Peabody had a dream that he lived in a two-dimensional town called Flatville. There were two-dimensional creatures in the town, all shaped like polygons.

Help Professor Peabody design a zoo for the creatures. Use the shapes on the *Shapes Zoo Pieces* Activity Page in the *Discovery Assignment Book*.

12. Decide on a way to classify the shapes on the *Shapes Zoo Pieces* Activity Page. Work with your class or your group to design and make a map of the Flatville Zoo.

13. Label each section of your zoo with the type of shape in that section.

14. Write a definition for each type of shape in your zoo.

15. Write a paragraph explaining the organization of your zoo.

214 SG · Grade 5 · Unit 6 · Lesson 6   Classifying Shapes

Student Guide **- page 214 *(Answers on p. 110)***

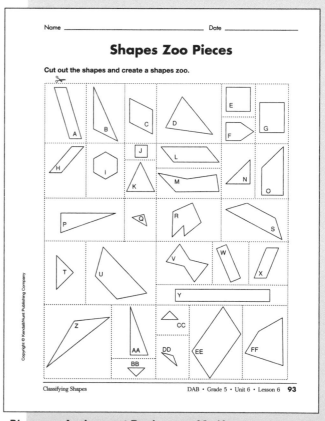

Discovery Assignment Book **- page 93 *(Answers on p. 112)***

One way of organizing the Zoo is shown in Figure 32.

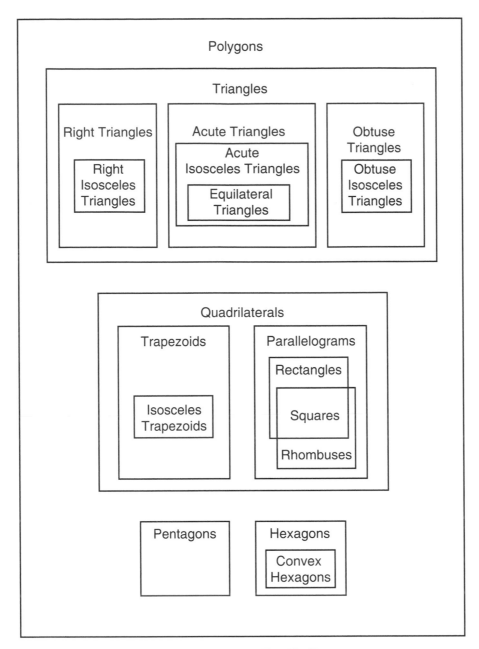

Figure 32: *A sample Flatville Zoo*

For easy reference, we include a dictionary for some common geometric terms below.

Geometry Terms

acute triangle: a triangle with all acute angles

isosceles triangle: a triangle with at least two sides the same length

obtuse triangle: a triangle with an obtuse angle

parallelogram: a quadrilateral with two pairs of parallel sides

rectangle: a quadrilateral with four right angles

rhombus: a quadrilateral with four sides of equal length (sometimes this is called a "diamond")

right triangle: a triangle with one right angle

square: a quadrilateral with four equal sides and four right angles

trapezoid: a quadrilateral with exactly one pair of parallel sides

Math Facts

DPP items O and P provide practice using the last six facts.

Homework and Practice

- Before students complete The Flatville Zoo section, assign the Homework section in the *Student Guide* and discuss the terms **parallelogram** and **convex** in class.

- Assign DPP Bit M for practice finding angle measures in triangles and Task N for practice solving problems with time and money.

- Assign Part 7 of the Home Practice, which includes word problems involving time.

Answers for Part 7 of the Home Practice are in the Answer Key at the end of this lesson and at the end of this unit.

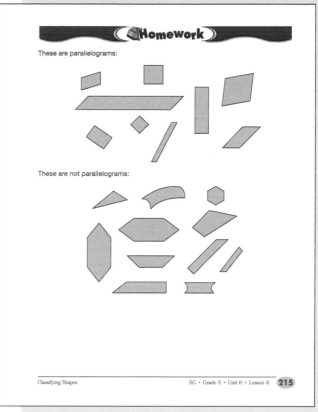

These are parallelograms:

These are not parallelograms:

Classifying Shapes   SG · Grade 5 · Unit 6 · Lesson 6   **215**

Student Guide - page 215

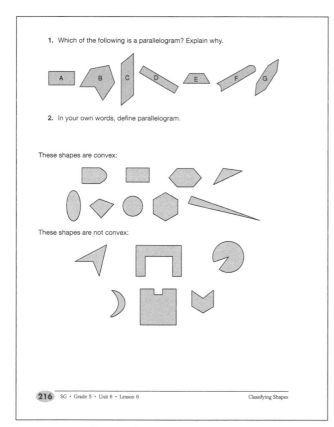

1. Which of the following is a parallelogram? Explain why.

2. In your own words, define parallelogram.

These shapes are convex:

These shapes are not convex:

216   SG · Grade 5 · Unit 6 · Lesson 6   Classifying Shapes

Student Guide - page 216 (Answers on p. 110)

3. Which of the following are convex? Explain why.

4. Define convex in your own words.

Classifying Shapes   SG · Grade 5 · Unit 6 · Lesson 6   **217**

Student Guide - page 217 (Answers on p. 111)

PART 7 Travel Time Problems

Choose an appropriate method to solve each of the following problems. For some questions you may need to find an exact answer, while for others you may only need an estimate. For each question, you may choose to use paper and pencil, mental math, or a calculator. Use a separate sheet of paper to show how you solved each problem.

1. John and his family are driving from Chicago, Illinois, to Phoenix, Arizona. His family plans to take 4 days to make this trip. Phoenix is 1776 miles from Chicago. About how many miles should they drive each of the four days if they want to drive about the same amount each day?

2. On the first day of the trip, John's family leaves home at 7:30 A.M. They drive for 4 hours before stopping to eat lunch. If they average 62 miles per hour, how far did they drive before stopping?

3. At the end of the second day of driving, John's family has traveled 957 miles and has spent $16\frac{1}{2}$ hours on the road. About how many miles per hour did they average so far on their trip?

4. One night John's family stops for pizza. They order a large pizza that is $\frac{1}{2}$ pepperoni and $\frac{1}{2}$ cheese. It is cut into 16 slices of the same size. If John eats one slice of pepperoni and one slice of cheese, what fraction of the pizza is this?

5. In Phoenix, John's family stays in a hotel for 7 nights. The hotel costs $97.00 per night including tax. What is the total bill for their 7-night stay?

6. When John's family arrives home, he calculates the number of gallons of gasoline they used during their trip to and from Phoenix. The car averages about 24 miles per gallon.

   A. How many gallons of gas did they use during the drive to and from Phoenix?

   B. If the average cost of gasoline is $1.57 per gallon, how much money did John's family spend on gasoline during the trip?

84 DAB • Grade 5 • Unit 6   GEOMETRY

Discovery Assignment Book - page 84 *(Answers on p. 111)*

Assessment

Use The Flatville Zoo section in the *Student Guide* as an assessment. Look for the following:

- Can students transfer the concept of a "classification tree" to the task of designing and organizing a zoo?

- Can they sort the Flatville shapes using geometric attributes?

- Can students describe their categories in words? (This is a higher-level task.)

Use this assessment to evaluate students' mathematical development, not mastery.

Extension

- Most zoos today organize by habitat, not anatomy. Ask students to design their own zoos based on habitat. They might first classify by geographical location (i.e., North or South America), then by climate (i.e., rainforest or desert), and then by where the animals live (i.e., underground or in trees). Again, there may be classifications that overlap.

- Assign DPP Challenge P, which asks students to use the last six facts in challenging problems.

Estimated Class Sessions 2-3

At a Glance

Math Facts and Daily Practice and Problems

Complete DPP items M–P for this lesson.

Part 1. Classification

1. Show students a classification tree for animals. One is provided on the *Classifying Shapes* Activity Pages in the *Student Guide.* Discuss how a tree is organized and how one defines various classes of animals.
2. Have students add other classes of animals to the tree (either as a class or in groups).
3. Show students a classification tree for geometric shapes. Discuss how a tree is organized and how one defines various classes of shapes.
4. Have students add other classes of polygons to the tree (either as a class or in groups).
5. Have students look at Professor Peabody's Zoo in the *Student Guide.* Discuss whether his organization makes sense. Discuss *Questions 8–11* in the *Student Guide.*

Part 2. The Flatville Zoo

1. Have students cut out the shapes on the *Shapes Zoo Pieces* Activity Page in the *Discovery Assignment Book.* They classify the shapes by sorting them and make a map of the Flatville Zoo. (See *Question 12* in the *Student Guide.*)
2. Students answer *Questions 13–15* in the *Student Guide.*

Homework

1. Assign the Homework section in the *Student Guide* before Part 2.
2. Assign Part 7 of the Home Practice.

Assessment

You can use The Flatville Zoo section in the *Student Guide* as an assessment.

Extension

1. Ask students to design their own zoos by habitat.
2. Assign DPP Challenge P.

Answer Key is on pages 108–112.

Notes:

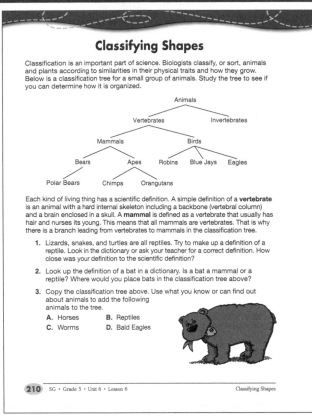

Student Guide - page 210

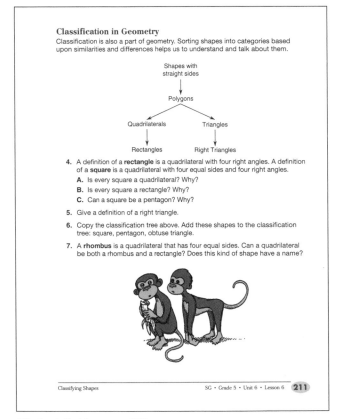

Student Guide - page 211

Student Guide (p. 210)

Classifying Shapes

1. Answers will vary. Reptiles are vertebrates whose bodies are usually covered with scales or bony plates. Their eggs, which are waterproof, are usually laid on land.

2. Bats are mammals, so bats would go under mammals with a separate line, like the lines for bears and apes.

3.

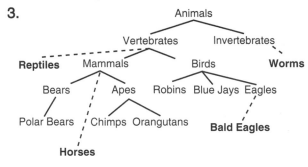

Student Guide (p. 211)

4. **A.** Yes, every square has four sides.

   B. Yes, every square has four right angles and opposite sides congruent.*

   C. No, every square has four sides not five.*

5. A triangle with one angle measurement of 90°.

6.

Shapes with straight sides

Polygons - - - - - - -> **Pentagon**

Quadrilaterals   Triangles

Rectangles   Right Triangles   **Obtuse Triangle**

Square

7. Yes, it is called a square.*

*Answers and/or discussion are included in the Lesson Guide.

Student Guide (pp. 212–213)

8. Professor Peabody organized the zoo so those with similar traits are close to each other.

9. Horses are vertebrates and mammals, but they are not elephants, apes, or bats. So horses would be a new subgroup in mammals. Hawks are vertebrates and birds and raptors. They are not eagles or owls, so they are a new section under raptors.

10. Professor Peabody's current classification scheme does not lend itself well to creating a new section for "Animals that Fly." To do this, Professor Peabody would need to include bats, all raptors, butterflies, and some ants. He could do this by creating a new section for Animals that Fly that overlaps with other sections. Bats, for example, could then be in both the Mammals section and the new section. The "zoo" discussed in Question 11 illustrates such an overlapping classification scheme.

11. **A.** Buffalo fit in D. Buffalo live in North America and are herbivores.

    B. Ostrich fits in A. It is an African omnivore.

    C. Coyote fits in C. It is a North American carnivore.

    D. African lion fits in B. It is both African and a carnivore.

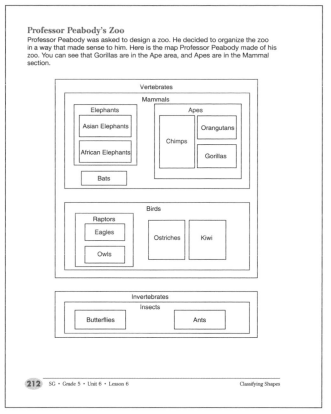

Student Guide - page 212

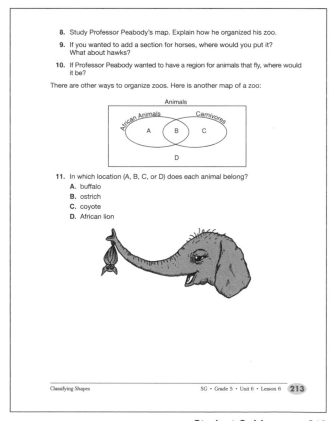

Student Guide - page 213

The Flatville Zoo

Professor Peabody had a dream that he lived in a two-dimensional town called Flatville. There were two-dimensional creatures in the town, all shaped like polygons.

Help Professor Peabody design a zoo for the creatures. Use the shapes on the *Shapes Zoo Pieces* Activity Page in the *Discovery Assignment Book*.

12. Decide on a way to classify the shapes on the *Shapes Zoo Pieces* Activity Page. Work with your class or your group to design and make a map of the Flatville Zoo.

13. Label each section of your zoo with the type of shape in that section.

14. Write a definition for each type of shape in your zoo.

15. Write a paragraph explaining the organization of your zoo.

Student Guide - page 214

Student Guide (pp. 214, 216)

12.–15. Answers will vary.

Homework

1. A, C, D

2. Definitions will vary. Students might say: A parallelogram is a shape that has four sides. Each pair of opposite sides are parallel. The sum of its interior angles is 360°.

---

1. Which of the following is a parallelogram? Explain why.

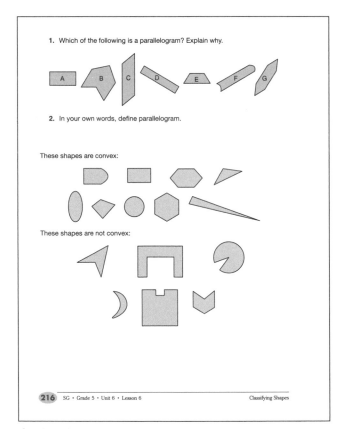

2. In your own words, define parallelogram.

These shapes are convex:

These shapes are not convex:

Student Guide - page 216

Student Guide (p. 217)

3. A, C, E, F, G

4. Definitions will vary. Students might say: A convex shape has no indents or does not "go in."

Discovery Assignment Book (p. 84)

Home Practice*

Part 7. Travel Time Problems

1. One possible answer is about 450 miles per day.

2. 248 miles

3. One possible answer is about 50 miles per hour ($1000 \div 20 = 50$).

4. $\frac{2}{16}$ or $\frac{1}{8}$

5. $609

6. Since the car averages about 24 miles per gallon, it is appropriate to answer both Questions 6A and 6B with an estimate.

   A. Three possible answers are: $1800 \div 20 = 90$ gallons, $1800 \div 30 = 60$ gallons, or an estimate between 60 gallons and 90 gallons.

   B. One possible answer is: 60 gallons $\times$ $1.50 = $90

*Answers for all the Home Practice in the *Discovery Assignment Book* are at the end of the unit.

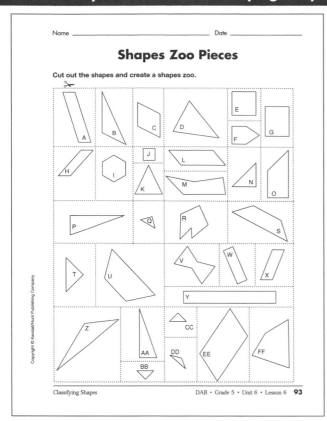

Discovery Assignment Book - **page 93**

Discovery Assignment Book (p. 93)

Shapes Zoo Pieces

Students' zoos will vary.

Lesson 7

Making Shapes

Estimated Class Sessions 1-2

Lesson Overview

In this activity, students draw two-dimensional shapes based on information given in an "order" for a slab of stone. The *Telling* rubric is used as a guide for exemplary work.

Key Content

- Constructing polygons with specific measurements (lengths of sides or angle measures).
- Constructing shapes with specified properties.
- Using geometric concepts and skills to solve problems.
- Communicating solutions orally and in writing.

Math Facts

Complete DPP item Q for this lesson. Item Q quizzes the last six facts.

Homework

1. Use uncompleted orders on the *Making Shapes* Activity Pages as homework.
2. Assign Part 5 of the Home Practice.

Assessment

1. Use the *Slab Orders* Assessment Page to assess students' understanding. Score **Question 4** on the *Telling* Rubric.
2. Transfer appropriate documentation from the Unit 6 *Observational Assessment Record* to students' *Individual Assessment Record Sheets*.

Curriculum Sequence

Before This Unit

Students were introduced to the *Telling* rubric in Unit 2.

After This Unit

Compasses will be used for constructions in Unit 14 *Using Circles*.

Materials List

Supplies and Copies

Student	Teacher
Supplies for Each Student • protractor • ruler • straws and chenille sticks, optional	**Supplies** • straws and chenille sticks, optional • overhead ruler • protractor
Copies • 1 copy of *Slab Orders* per student (*Unit Resource Guide* Page 120)	**Copies/Transparencies** • 1 copy of *TIMS Multidimensional Rubric* (*Teacher Implementation Guide,* Assessment section) • 1 transparency or poster of Student Rubric: *Telling* (*Teacher Implementation Guide,* Assessment section)

All blackline masters including assessment, transparency, and DPP masters are also on the Teacher Resource CD.

Student Books
Making Shapes (*Student Guide* Pages 218–219)
Student Rubric: *Telling* (*Student Guide* Appendix C and Inside Back Cover)

Daily Practice and Problems and Home Practice
DPP items Q–R (*Unit Resource Guide* Pages 25–26)
Home Practice Part 5 (*Discovery Assignment Book* Page 83)

Note: Classrooms whose pacing differs significantly from the suggested pacing of the units should use the Math Facts Calendar in Section 4 of the *Facts Resource Guide* to ensure students receive the complete math facts program.

Assessment Tools
TIMS Multidimensional Rubric (*Teacher Implementation Guide,* Assessment section)
Observational Assessment Record (*Unit Resource Guide* Pages 11–12)
Individual Assessment Record Sheet (*Teacher Implementation Guide,* Assessment section)

Daily Practice and Problems

Suggestions for using the DPPs are on page 118.

Q. Bit: Quiz: The Last Six Facts (URG p. 25)

A. $6 \times 7 =$

B. $24 \div 6 =$

C. $8 \times 7 =$

D. $7 \times 4 =$

E. $48 \div 8 =$

F. $32 \div 4 =$

R. Challenge: Is It Possible?
(URG p. 26)

You may need to experiment to find these answers. Explain your answers in words or pictures.

1. Can a triangle have two right angles?
2. If two angles of a triangle are equal, does the third angle also have to be equal to the other two angles?
3. If a triangle has two equal sides, can its angles all be different sizes?

Student Guide - page 218 *(Answers on p. 121)*

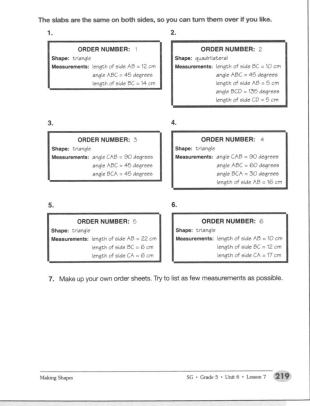

Student Guide - page 219 *(Answers on p. 121)*

Teaching the Activity

Introduce students to the imaginary setting for this activity by having them read and discuss the *Making Shapes* Activity Pages in the *Student Guide.* They will be given "orders" to make polygons meeting certain specifications. Their task is to draw the polygon, if possible. Sometimes the order will be impossible to fill, sometimes there will be exactly one way to fill the order, and sometimes there will be two or more ways to fill the order. Have students work independently, in pairs, or in small groups to solve the problems. If they work in groups, they should write up their solutions independently.

You might start by doing one example with the whole class. Example:

Shape: triangle ABC
Measurements: length of side AB = 10 cm
∠A = 60 degrees
length of side AC = 20 cm

You can draw angle CAB first and then mark off the lengths of the two sides AB and AC. Most students will probably carry out the steps in the order that the three measurements are given, drawing side AB using a pencil and a ruler, drawing a 60-degree angle at CAB, marking off 20 cm on AC, and finally connecting B to C. The third side should turn out to be a little more than 17 cm long. All solutions are congruent. Have them show this by sliding and turning one student's triangle until it is on top of another. You may also need to "flip" one of the triangles. This is the reason that we made the "slabs" the same on both sides. Students should complete the orders on the *Making Shapes* Activity Pages in the *Student Guide.*

Question 6 on the *Making Shapes* Activity Pages is a bit tricky. Students can easily draw one side of the triangle, but may have difficulty drawing the second side, since they don't know the angle between AB and BC. Students encountered a similar problem in Lesson 4. One way to fill this order, other than trial and error, is to cut three straws into lengths of 10, 12, and 17 cm and connect them with chenille sticks. This should produce a triangle pretty close to what we wanted. Now mark the vertices on paper and connect the vertices with straight lines.

Have students sketch their shapes lightly in pencil. Once they check that their shape is correct, they can go over it in darker pencil or pen. Make sure students draw only the shapes needed, and not a three-dimensional representation.

Another method that does not rely on special items like straws is to draw one of the sides, such as side AB. Then, slide around two rulers, one touching the 17 cm mark (A) and the other touching the 12 cm mark (B), until sides of the correct length are made (see Figure 33). Make a dot where the two rulers meet and label this point C. Finally, you can draw the line segments AC and BC. A third method is to mark off a 12-cm length on the edge of one piece of paper and a 17-cm length on the edge of a second piece of paper. Then, slide around the pieces of paper to locate the point C.

Now give students four "orders" on the *Slab Orders* Assessment Page in the *Unit Resource Guide*. Before students begin, advise them that you will score their work for **Question 4** using the guidelines in the *Telling* Student Rubric. Review with students the *Telling* Rubric from Appendix C or inside back cover in the *Student Guide* so they will know what you expect.

Grade **Question 4** on the *Slab Orders* Assessment Page using the Telling dimension of the *TIMS Multidimensional Rubric*. Note that directions for the slab order are not given in the most convenient order. To assist you in scoring students' work using this dimension, questions specific to this task are listed below:

Telling

- Did students give a clear description of the process they used to solve the problem?
- Did students explain with pictures or diagrams how they arrived at their solutions?
- Did students use geometric terms correctly?
- Did students support their solution with previous mathematical experiences?

TIMS Tip

Students might also know how to construct this shape using a compass and arcs. Encourage them to use a compass if they are familiar with this tool. Compasses will be used for constructions in Unit 14.

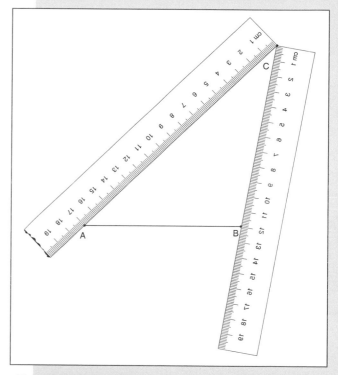

Figure 33: *Using two rulers to draw a triangle with sides 10, 12, and 17 cm*

Journal Prompt

A triangle has six parts that can be measured—three sides and three angles. Do you need all six measurements to be able to build the triangle? Which measurements are enough to build a triangle?

PART 5 **Slab-Maker Problems**

Draw these shapes and answer the questions on a separate sheet of paper.
You will need a centimeter ruler and a protractor.

1. Draw triangle DEF. The length of side EF is 5 cm. Angle F is a right angle. The length of DF is 12 cm. What is the length of side DE?

2. Draw rectangle GHIJ. The length of GH is 8 cm. The length of HI is half the length of GH. What is the area of this rectangle?

3. Draw quadrilateral QRST. The length of ST is 6 cm. Angles S and T are both 60°. The lengths of sides RS and QT are 2 cm. Which two line segments are parallel?

4. Draw a pentagon with two right angles. Have one side measure 4 cm and one side measure 5 cm. Do you think everyone will draw congruent pentagons? How do you know?

PART 6 **Fractions**

1. Solve the following addition and subtraction problems.

    A. $\frac{1}{2} + \frac{5}{8} =$ _____

    B. $\frac{2}{3} + \frac{1}{12} =$ _____

    C. $\frac{7}{12} - \frac{1}{2} =$ _____

    D. $\frac{3}{5} - \frac{3}{10} =$ _____

2. Draw pictures to help you answer these questions. You may use dot paper to help you.

    A. One furlong is $\frac{1}{8}$ mile. How many furlongs equal one mile?

    B. A tablespoon is $\frac{1}{16}$ of a cup. How many tablespoons equal one cup?

    C. One foot is $\frac{1}{3}$ of a yard. How many feet equal one yard?

    D. Five minutes is $\frac{1}{12}$ of an hour. How many minutes equal $\frac{3}{12}$ of an hour?

    E. Gold that is pure is called 24 karat gold. If 1 out of 24 parts is pure, it is 1 karat gold. Gold that is 10 karat is $\frac{10}{24}$ or $\frac{5}{12}$ pure. Is 14 karat gold more or less than $\frac{1}{2}$ pure gold?

GEOMETRY   DAB • Grade 5 • Unit 6   **83**

Discovery Assignment Book - page 83 (Answers on p. 122)

Math Facts

DPP item Q quizzes the last six facts. After taking the quiz, students update their *Facts I Know* charts.

Homework and Practice

- Use orders not completed on the *Making Shapes* Activity Pages in the *Student Guide* as homework.

- Assign Part 5 of the Home Practice, which involves more slab-maker problems.

Answers for Part 5 of the Home Practice are in the Answer Key at the end of this lesson and at the end of this unit.

Assessment

- Use the *Slab Orders* Assessment Page.

- Transfer appropriate documentation from the Unit 6 *Observational Assessment Record* to students' *Individual Assessment Record Sheets*.

Extension

- Have students work in at least two small groups to make up their own problems. The groups then exchange problems and each group solves other groups' problems. Give extra credit for groups that specify a shape using the minimum number of clues. Challenge students to make up diverse types of problems.

- Use DPP Challenge R to extend students' reasoning and communication skills.

At a Glance

Math Facts and Daily Practice and Problems

Complete DPP items Q–R for this lesson. Item Q quizzes the last six facts.

Teaching the Activity

1. Present the *Making Shapes* Activity Pages in the *Student Guide.*
2. Do the example in the Lesson Guide with the class to make sure they understand the task.
3. Have students work individually or in small groups to solve the orders in *Questions 1–7* on the *Making Shapes* Activity Pages in the *Student Guide.*
4. Have students read and discuss the *Student Guide* pages for the Student Rubric *Telling.*

Homework

1. Use uncompleted orders on the *Making Shapes* Activity Pages as homework.
2. Assign Part 5 of the Home Practice.

Assessment

1. Use the *Slab Orders* Assessment Page to assess students' understanding. Score *Question 4* on the *Telling* Rubric.
2. Transfer appropriate documentation from the Unit 6 *Observational Assessment Record* to students' *Individual Assessment Record Sheets.*

Extension

1. Have students make up their own problems.
2. Assign DPP Challenge R.

Answer Key is on pages 121–123.

Notes:

Slab Orders

Complete the following orders. If an order is impossible to fill, say so. If an order has more than one solution, give at least two solutions. Use the *Telling* rubric to help you describe the process you used to complete each order.

1.

ORDER NUMBER: 1

Shape: triangle

Measurements: length of side AB = 12 cm
angle BAC = 90 degrees
length of side AC = 16 cm

2.

ORDER NUMBER: 2

Shape: rectangle

Measurements: length of side AB = 18 cm
length of side BC = 9 cm

3.

ORDER NUMBER: 3

Shape: rectangle

Measurements: length of side AB = 10 cm
length of side BC = 12 cm
length of side CD = 14 cm
length of side DA = 12 cm

4.

ORDER NUMBER: 4

Shape: trapezoid

Measurements: length of side AB = 15 cm
length of side CD = 10 cm
angle ABC = 60 degrees
length of side BC = 6 cm

Assessment Blackline Master

Student Guide (pp. 218–219)

Making Shapes

1.

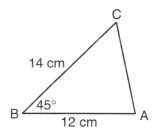

2.

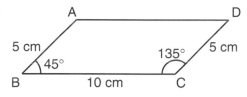

3. Two possible solutions are shown. There are many possible solutions that are similar to one another.

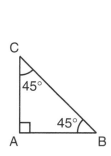 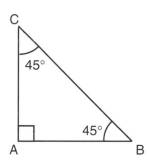

4.

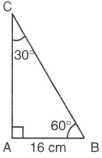

5. Impossible; the two shorter sides of a triangle must sum to be larger than the third side.

6.

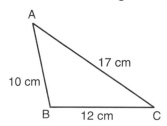

7. Order sheets will vary.

Student Guide - page 218

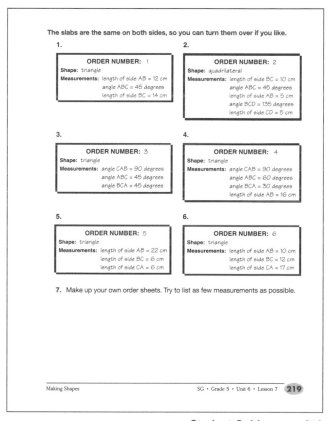

Student Guide - page 219

PART 5 Slab-Maker Problems

Draw these shapes and answer the questions on a separate sheet of paper.
You will need a centimeter ruler and a protractor.

1. Draw triangle DEF. The length of side EF is 5 cm. Angle F is a right angle. The length of DF is 12 cm. What is the length of side DE?

2. Draw rectangle GHIJ. The length of GH is 8 cm. The length of HI is half the length of GH. What is the area of this rectangle?

3. Draw quadrilateral QRST. The length of ST is 6 cm. Angles S and T are both 60°. The lengths of sides RS and QT are 2 cm. Which two line segments are parallel?

4. Draw a pentagon with two right angles. Have one side measure 4 cm and one side measure 5 cm. Do you think everyone will draw congruent pentagons? How do you know?

PART 6 Fractions

1. Solve the following addition and subtraction problems.

   A. $\frac{1}{2} + \frac{5}{8} =$ _____   B. $\frac{2}{3} + \frac{1}{12} =$ _____

   C. $\frac{7}{12} - \frac{1}{2} =$ _____   D. $\frac{3}{5} - \frac{3}{10} =$ _____

2. Draw pictures to help you answer these questions. You may use dot paper to help you.

   A. One furlong is $\frac{1}{8}$ mile. How many furlongs equal one mile?

   B. A tablespoon is $\frac{1}{16}$ of a cup. How many tablespoons equal one cup?

   C. One foot is $\frac{1}{3}$ of a yard. How many feet equal one yard?

   D. Five minutes is $\frac{1}{12}$ of an hour. How many minutes equal $\frac{3}{12}$ of an hour?

   E. Gold that is pure is called 24 karat gold. If 1 out of 24 parts is pure, it is 1 karat gold. Gold that is 10 karat is $\frac{10}{24}$ or $\frac{5}{12}$ pure. Is 14 karat gold more or less than $\frac{1}{2}$ pure gold?

GEOMETRY   DAB • Grade 5 • Unit 6   **83**

Discovery Assignment Book - page 83

Discovery Assignment Book (p. 83)

Home Practice*

Part 5. Slab-Maker Problems

1. 13 cm

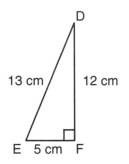

2. 32 square centimeters

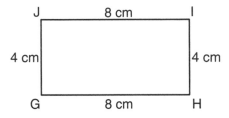

3. sides RQ and ST are parallel

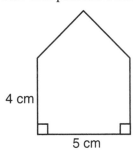

4. No. One possible solution is shown.

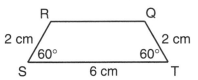

*Answers for all the Home Practice in the *Discovery Assignment Book* are at the end of the unit.

Unit Resource Guide (p. 120)

Slab Orders

1.

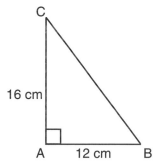

2.

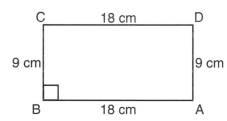

3. Impossible, opposite sides are congruent in a rectangle.

4.

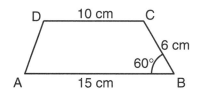

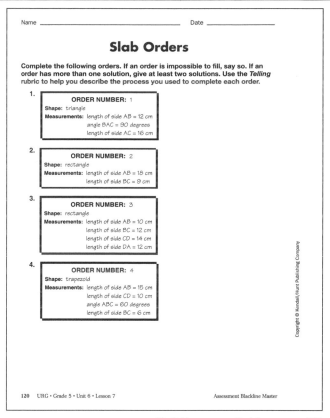

Unit Resource Guide - page 120

Name _____ Date _____

Unit 6 Home Practice

PART 1 Triangle Flash Cards: Last Six Facts
Study for the quiz on the multiplication and division facts for the last six facts
(4×6, 4×7, 4×8, 6×7, 6×8, and 7×8). Take home your *Triangle Flash Cards: Last Six Facts* and your list of facts you need to study.

Ask a family member to choose one flash card at a time. To quiz you on a multiplication fact, he or she should cover the corner containing the highest number. Multiply the two uncovered numbers.

To quiz you on a division fact, your family member can cover one of the smaller numbers. One of the smaller numbers is circled. The other has a square around it. Use the two uncovered numbers to solve a division fact.

Ask your family member to mix up the multiplication and division facts. He or she should sometimes cover the highest number, sometimes cover the circled number, and sometimes cover the number in the square.

Your teacher will tell you when the quiz on the last six facts will be given.

PART 2 Practicing Addition and Subtraction
Use paper and pencil to solve the following problems. Estimate to be sure your answers are reasonable. Use a separate sheet of paper, if you need more work space.

A. $549 + 82 =$ _____ B. $629 - 347 =$ _____ C. $843 + 178 =$ _____

D. $213 - 58 =$ _____ E. $7542 + 282 =$ _____ F. $1067 + 93 =$ _____

G. $4057 - 492 =$ _____ H. $2715 + 206 =$ _____ I. $462 - 379 =$ _____

GEOMETRY   DAB • Grade 5 • Unit 6   **81**

Discovery Assignment Book - page 81

Name _____ Date _____

PART 3 Angles and Triangles
You will need a protractor to complete this section. Use the straight edge on your protractor to draw the angles and triangle in Questions 1, 2, and 4.

1. On a separate sheet of paper, draw an angle that is greater than 90°. Name the angle YTV. Then measure the angle to the nearest degree.

2. On a separate sheet of paper, draw an angle that is less than 45°. Name the angle RGM. Then measure the angle to the nearest degree.

3. If triangle ADK has two angles that are 40° each, what is the measure of the third angle? How do you know?

4. Can a triangle have two 70° angles and one that measures 50°? How do you know?

5. One angle in triangle QFP is a right angle. A second angle is 27°. What is the measure of the third angle? How do you know?

6. One angle in a triangle measures 32°. Another angle is twice as large. What is the measure of the third angle? How do you know?

PART 4 Practicing Multiplication and Division
Use paper and pencil to solve the following problems. Estimate to be sure your answers are reasonable. Use a separate sheet of paper to show your work.

A. $607 \times 8 =$ _____ B. $174 \times 9 =$ _____ C. $435 \div 3 =$ _____

D. $420 \div 9 =$ _____ E. $4631 \times 5 =$ _____ F. $768 \div 5 =$ _____

G. $68 \times 34 =$ _____ H. $577 \div 7 =$ _____ I. $1652 \div 4 =$ _____

82 DAB • Grade 5 • Unit 6   GEOMETRY

Discovery Assignment Book - page 82

Discovery Assignment Book (p. 81)

Part 2. Practicing Addition and Subtraction

A. 631   B. 282

C. 1021   D. 155

E. 7824   F. 1160

G. 3565   H. 2921

I. 83

Discovery Assignment Book (p. 82)

Part 3. Angles and Triangles

1. Angles will vary. One possible angle is shown.

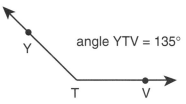

angle YTV = 135°

2. Angles will vary. One possible angle is shown.

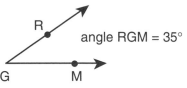

angle RGM = 35°

3. $100°$; $40° + 40° = 80°$; $180° - 80° = 100°$

4. No; $70° + 70° + 50° = 190°$.

5. $180° - 27° - 90° = 63°$.

6. $32° + (32° \times 2) = 96°$; $180° - 96° = 84°$.

Part 4. Practicing Multiplication and Division

A. 4856   B. 1566

C. 145   D. 46 R6

E. 23,155   F. 153 R3

G. 2312   H. 82 R3

I. 413

Discovery Assignment Book (p. 83)

Part 5. Slab-Maker Problems

1. 13 cm

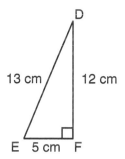

2. 32 square centimeters

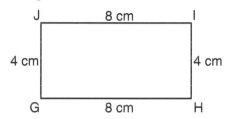

3. sides RQ and ST are parallel

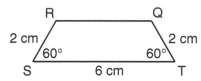

4. No. One possible solution is shown.

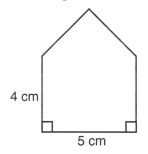

Part 6. Fractions

1. **A.** $\frac{9}{8}$

   B. $\frac{9}{12}$ or $\frac{3}{4}$

   C. $\frac{1}{12}$

   D. $\frac{3}{10}$

2. **A.** 8 furlongs

   B. 16 tablespoons

   C. 3 feet

   D. 15 minutes

   E. more

Discovery Assignment Book - page 83

PART 7 Travel Time Problems

Choose an appropriate method to solve each of the following problems. For some questions you may need to find an exact answer, while for others you may only need an estimate. For each question, you may choose to use paper and pencil, mental math, or a calculator. Use a separate sheet of paper to show how you solved each problem.

1. John and his family are driving from Chicago, Illinois, to Phoenix, Arizona. His family plans to take 4 days to make this trip. Phoenix is 1776 miles from Chicago. About how many miles should they drive each of the four days if they want to drive about the same amount each day?

2. On the first day of the trip, John's family leaves home at 7:30 A.M. They drive for 4 hours before stopping to eat lunch. If they average 62 miles per hour, how far did they drive before stopping?

3. At the end of the second day of driving, John's family has traveled 957 miles and has spent $16\frac{1}{2}$ hours on the road. About how many miles per hour did they average so far on their trip?

4. One night John's family stops for pizza. They order a large pizza that is $\frac{1}{2}$ pepperoni and $\frac{1}{2}$ cheese. It is cut into 16 slices of the same size. If John eats one slice of pepperoni and one slice of cheese, what fraction of the pizza is this?

5. In Phoenix, John's family stays in a hotel for 7 nights. The hotel costs $97.00 per night including tax. What is the total bill for their 7-night stay?

6. When John's family arrives home, he calculates the number of gallons of gasoline they used during their trip to and from Phoenix. The car averages about 24 miles per gallon.
   A. How many gallons of gas did they use during the drive to and from Phoenix?

   B. If the average cost of gasoline is $1.57 per gallon, how much money did John's family spend on gasoline during the trip?

84 DAB • Grade 5 • Unit 6   GEOMETRY

Discovery Assignment Book - page 84

Discovery Assignment Book (p. 84)

Part 7. Travel Time Problems

1. One possible answer is about 450 miles per day.

2. 248 miles

3. One possible answer is about 50 miles per hour ($1000 \div 20 = 50$).

4. $\frac{2}{16}$ or $\frac{1}{8}$

5. $609

6. Since the car averages about 24 miles per gallon, it is appropriate to answer both Questions 6A and 6B with an estimate.

   A. Three possible answers are: $1800 \div 20 = 90$ gallons, $1800 \div 30 = 60$ gallons, or an estimate between 60 gallons and 90 gallons.

   B. One possible answer is: 60 gallons $\times$ $1.50 = $90.

Glossary

This glossary provides definitions of key vocabulary terms in the Grade 5 lessons. Locations of key vocabulary terms in the curriculum are included with each definition. Components Key: URG = *Unit Resource Guide* and SG = *Student Guide*.

A

Acute Angle (URG Unit 6; SG Unit 6)
An angle that measures less than 90°.

Acute Triangle (URG Unit 6 & Unit 15; SG Unit 6 & Unit 15)
A triangle that has only acute angles.

All-Partials Multiplication Method (URG Unit 2)
A paper-and-pencil method for solving multiplication problems. Each partial product is recorded on a separate line. (*See also* partial product.)

$$
\begin{array}{r}
186 \\
\times\ 3 \\
\hline
18 \\
240 \\
300 \\
\hline
558
\end{array}
$$

Altitude of a Triangle (URG Unit 15; SG Unit 15)
A line segment from a vertex of a triangle perpendicular to the opposite side or to the line extending the opposite side; also, the length of this line. The altitude is also called the height of the triangle.

Angle (URG Unit 6; SG Unit 6)
The amount of turning or the amount of opening between two rays that have the same endpoint.

Arc (URG Unit 14; SG Unit 14)
Part of a circle between two points. (*See also* circle.)

Area (URG Unit 4 & Unit 15; SG Unit 4 & Unit 15)
A measurement of size. The area of a shape is the amount of space it covers, measured in square units.

Average (URG Unit 1 & Unit 4; SG Unit 1 & Unit 4)
A number that can be used to represent a typical value in a set of data. (*See also* mean, median, and mode.)

Axes (URG Unit 10; SG Unit 10)
Reference lines on a graph. In the Cartesian coordinate system, the axes are two perpendicular lines that meet at the origin. The singular of axes is axis.

B

Base of a Triangle (URG Unit 15; SG Unit 15)
One of the sides of a triangle; also, the length of the side. A perpendicular line drawn from the vertex opposite the base is called the height or altitude of the triangle.

Base of an Exponent (URG Unit 2; SG Unit 2)
When exponents are used, the number being multiplied. In $3^4 = 3 \times 3 \times 3 \times 3 = 81$, the 3 is the base and the 4 is the exponent. The 3 is multiplied by itself 4 times.

Base-Ten Pieces (URG Unit 2; SG Unit 2)
A set of manipulatives used to model our number system as shown in the figure below. Note that a skinny is made of 10 bits, a flat is made of 100 bits, and a pack is made of 1000 bits.

Base-Ten Shorthand (URG Unit 2)
A graphical representation of the base-ten pieces as shown below.

Nickname	Picture	Shorthand
bit		
skinny	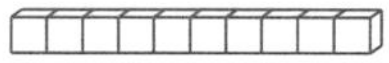	
flat	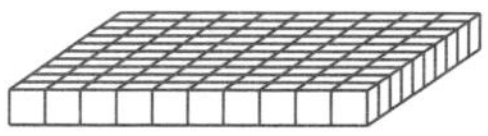	
pack	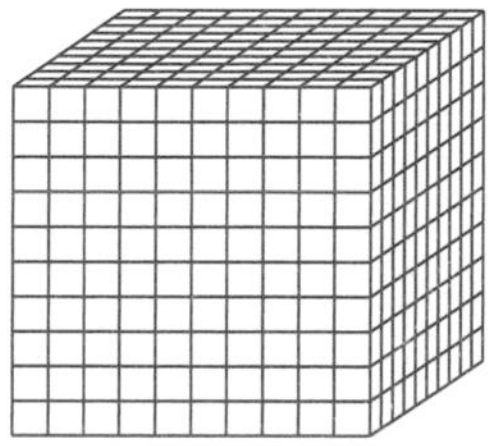	

Benchmarks (SG Unit 7)
Numbers convenient for comparing and ordering numbers, e.g., $0, \frac{1}{2}$, 1 are convenient benchmarks for comparing and ordering fractions.

Best-Fit Line (URG Unit 3; SG Unit 3)
The line that comes closest to the points on a point graph.

Binning Data (URG Unit 8; SG Unit 8)
Placing data from a data set with a large number of values or large range into intervals in order to more easily see patterns in the data.

Bit (URG Unit 2; SG Unit 2)
A cube that measures 1 cm on each edge.
It is the smallest of the base-ten pieces and is often used to represent 1. (*See also* base-ten pieces.)

C

Cartesian Coordinate System (URG Unit 10; SG Unit 10)
A method of locating points on a flat surface by means of an ordered pair of numbers. This method is named after its originator, René Descartes. (*See also* coordinates.)

Categorical Variable (URG Unit 1; SG Unit 1)
Variables with values that are not numbers. (*See also* variable and value.)

Center of a Circle (URG Unit 14; SG Unit 14)
The point such that every point on a circle is the same distance from it. (*See also* circle.)

Centiwheel (URG Unit 7; SG Unit 7)
A circle divided into 100 equal sections used in exploring fractions, decimals, and percents.

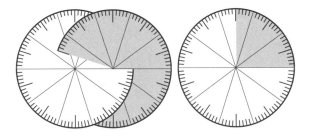

Central Angle (URG Unit 14; SG Unit 14)
An angle whose vertex is at the center of a circle.

Certain Event (URG Unit 7; SG Unit 7)
An event that has a probability of 1 (100%).

Chord (URG Unit 14; SG Unit 14)
A line segment that connects two points on a circle. (*See also* circle.)

Circle (URG Unit 14; SG Unit 14)
A curve that is made up of all the points that are the same distance from one point, the center.

Circumference (URG Unit 14; SG Unit 14)
The distance around a circle.

Common Denominator (URG Unit 5 & Unit 11; SG Unit 5 & Unit 11)
A denominator that is shared by two or more fractions. A common denominator is a common multiple of the denominators of the fractions. 15 is a common denominator of $\frac{2}{3}$ ($= \frac{10}{15}$) and $\frac{4}{5}$ ($= \frac{12}{15}$) since 15 is divisible by both 3 and 5.

Common Fraction (URG Unit 7; SG Unit 7)
Any fraction that is written with a numerator and denominator that are whole numbers. For example, $\frac{3}{4}$ and $\frac{9}{4}$ are both common fractions. (*See also* decimal fraction.)

Commutative Property of Addition (URG Unit 2)
The order of the addends in an addition problem does not matter, e.g., $7 + 3 = 3 + 7$.

Commutative Property of Multiplication (URG Unit 2)
The order of the factors in a multiplication problem does not matter, e.g., $7 \times 3 = 3 \times 7$. (*See also* turn-around facts.)

Compact Method (URG Unit 2)
Another name for what is considered the traditional multiplication algorithm.

$$\begin{array}{r} {}^{2\,1}186 \\ \times\ 3 \\ \hline 558 \end{array}$$

Composite Number (URG Unit 11; SG Unit 11)
A number that has more than two distinct factors. For example, 9 has three factors (1, 3, 9) so it is a composite number.

Concentric Circles (URG Unit 14; SG Unit 14)
Circles that have the same center.

Congruent (URG Unit 6 & Unit 10; SG Unit 6)
Figures that are the same shape and size. Polygons are congruent when corresponding sides have the same length and corresponding angles have the same measure.

Conjecture (URG Unit 11; SG Unit 11)
A statement that has not been proved to be true, nor shown to be false.

Convenient Number (URG Unit 2; SG Unit 2)
A number used in computation that is close enough to give a good estimate, but is also easy to compute with mentally, e.g., 25 and 30 are convenient numbers for 27.

Convex (URG Unit 6)
A shape is convex if for any two points in the shape, the line segment between the points is also inside the shape.

Coordinates (URG Unit 10; SG Unit 10)
An ordered pair of numbers that locates points on a flat surface relative to a pair of coordinate axes. For example, in the ordered pair (4, 5), the first number (coordinate) is the distance from the point to the vertical axis and the second coordinate is the distance from the point to the horizontal axis. (*See also* axes.)

Corresponding Parts (URG Unit 10; SG Unit 10)
Matching parts in two or more figures. In the figure
below, Sides AB and A′B′ are corresponding parts.

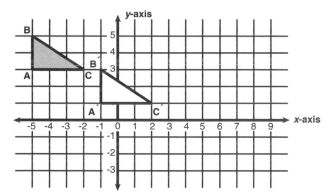

Cryptography (SG Unit 11) The study of secret codes.

Cubic Centimeter (URG Unit 13)
The volume of a cube that is one centimeter long on
each edge.

D

Data (SG Unit 1)
Information collected in an experiment or survey.

Decagon (URG Unit 6; SG Unit 6)
A ten-sided, ten-angled polygon.

Decimal (URG Unit 7; SG Unit 7)
1. A number written using the base ten place value
   system.
2. A number containing a decimal point.

Decimal Fraction (URG Unit 7; SG Unit 7)
A fraction written as a decimal. For example, 0.75 and
0.4 are decimal fractions and $\frac{75}{100}$ and $\frac{4}{10}$ are the equivalent
common fractions.

Degree (URG Unit 6; SG Unit 6)
A degree (°) is a unit of measure for angles. There are
360 degrees in a circle.

Denominator (URG Unit 3; SG Unit 3)
The number below the line in a fraction. The denominator indicates the number of equal parts in which the unit
whole is divided. For example, the 5 is the denominator
in the fraction $\frac{2}{5}$. In this case the unit whole is divided into
five equal parts. (*See also* numerator.)

Density (URG Unit 13; SG Unit 13)
The ratio of an object's mass to its volume.

Diagonal (URG Unit 6)
A line segment that connects nonadjacent corners of
a polygon.

Diameter (URG Unit 14; SG Unit 14)
1. A line segment that connects two points on a circle
   and passes through the center.
2. The length of this line segment.

Digit (SG Unit 2)
Any one of the ten symbols 0, 1, 2, 3, 4, 5, 6, 7, 8, 9.
The number 37 is made up of the digits 3 and 7.

Dividend (URG Unit 4 & Unit 9; SG Unit 4 & Unit 9)
The number that is divided in a division problem,
e.g., 12 is the dividend in 12 ÷ 3 = 4.

Divisor (URG Unit 2, Unit 4, & Unit 9; SG Unit 2,
    Unit 4, & Unit 9)
In a division problem, the number by which another
number is divided. In the problem 12 ÷ 4 = 3, the 4
is the divisor, the 12 is the dividend, and the 3 is the
quotient.

Dodecagon (URG Unit 6; SG Unit 6)
A twelve-sided, twelve-angled polygon.

E

Endpoint (URG Unit 6; SG Unit 6)
The point at either end of a line segment or the point at
the end of a ray.

Equally Likely (URG Unit 7; SG Unit 7)
When events have the same probability, they are called
equally likely.

Equidistant (URG Unit 14)
At the same distance.

Equilateral Triangle (URG Unit 6, Unit 14, & Unit 15)
A triangle that has all three sides equal in length. An
equilateral triangle also has three equal angles.

Equivalent Fractions (URG Unit 3; SG Unit 3)
Fractions that have the same value, e.g., $\frac{2}{4} = \frac{1}{2}$.

Estimate (URG Unit 2; SG Unit 2)
1. To find *about* how many (as a verb).
2. A number that is *close to* the desired number (as a
   noun).

Expanded Form (SG Unit 2)
A way to write numbers that shows the place value of
each digit, e.g., 4357 = 4000 + 300 + 50 + 7.

Exponent (URG Unit 2 & Unit 11; SG Unit 2 & Unit 11)
The number of times the base is multiplied by itself.
In $3^4 = 3 \times 3 \times 3 \times 3 = 81$, the 3 is the base and the
4 is the exponent. The 3 is multiplied by itself 4 times.

Extrapolation (URG Unit 13; SG Unit 13)
Using patterns in data to make predictions or to estimate
values that lie beyond the range of values in the set of
data.

F

Fact Families (URG Unit 2; SG Unit 2)
Related math facts, e.g., 3 × 4 = 12, 4 × 3 = 12,
12 ÷ 3 = 4, 12 ÷ 4 = 3.

Factor Tree (URG Unit 11; SG Unit 11)
A diagram that shows the prime factorization of a number.

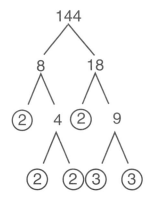

Factors (URG Unit 2 & Unit 11; SG Unit 2 & Unit 11)
1. In a multiplication problem, the numbers that are multiplied together. In the problem $3 \times 4 = 12$, 3 and 4 are the factors.
2. Numbers that divide a number evenly, e.g., 1, 2, 3, 4, 6, and 12 are all the factors of 12.

Fair Game (URG Unit 7; SG Unit 7)
A game in which it is equally likely that any player will win.

Fewest Pieces Rule (URG Unit 2)
Using the least number of base-ten pieces to represent a number. (*See also* base-ten pieces.)

Fixed Variables (URG Unit 4; SG Unit 3 & Unit 4)
Variables in an experiment that are held constant or not changed, in order to find the relationship between the manipulated and responding variables. These variables are often called controlled variables. (*See also* manipulated variable and responding variable.)

Flat (URG Unit 2; SG Unit 2)
A block that measures 1 cm $\times$ 10 cm $\times$ 10 cm. It is one of the base-ten pieces and is often used to represent 100. (*See also* base-ten pieces.)

Flip (URG Unit 10; SG Unit 10)
A motion of the plane in which the plane is reflected over a line so that any point and its image are the same distance from the line.

Forgiving Division Method
(URG Unit 4; SG Unit 4)
A paper-and-pencil method for division in which successive partial quotients are chosen and subtracted from the dividend, until the remainder is less than the divisor. The sum of the partial quotients is the quotient. For example, $644 \div 7$ can be solved as shown at the right.

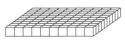

Formula (SG Unit 11 & Unit 14)
A number sentence that gives a general rule. A formula for finding the area of a rectangle is Area = length $\times$ width, or $A = l \times w$.

Fraction (URG Unit 7; SG Unit 7)
A number that can be written as a/b where a and b are whole numbers and b is not zero.

G

Googol (URG Unit 2)
A number that is written as a 1 with 100 zeroes after it (10^{100}).

Googolplex (URG Unit 2)
A number that is written as a 1 with a googol of zeroes after it.

H

Height of a Triangle (URG Unit 15; SG Unit 15)
A line segment from a vertex of a triangle perpendicular to the opposite side or to the line extending the opposite side; also, the length of this line. The height is also called the altitude.

Hexagon (URG Unit 6; SG Unit 6)
A six-sided polygon.

Hypotenuse (URG Unit 15; SG Unit 15)
The longest side of a right triangle.

I

Image (URG Unit 10; SG Unit 10)
The result of a transformation, in particular a slide (translation) or a flip (reflection), in a coordinate plane. The new figure after the slide or flip is the image of the old figure.

Impossible Event (URG Unit 7; SG Unit 7)
An event that has a probability of 0 or 0%.

Improper Fraction (URG Unit 3; SG Unit 3)
A fraction in which the numerator is greater than or equal to the denominator. An improper fraction is greater than or equal to one.

Infinite (URG Unit 2)
Never ending, immeasurably great, unlimited.

Interpolation (URG Unit 13; SG Unit 13)
Making predictions or estimating values that lie between data points in a set of data.

Intersect (URG Unit 14)
To meet or cross.

Isosceles Triangle (URG Unit 6 & Unit 15)
A triangle that has at least two sides of equal length.

J

K

L

Lattice Multiplication
(URG Unit 9; SG Unit 9)
A method for multiplying that
uses a lattice to arrange the
partial products so the digits are
correctly placed in the correct
place value columns. A lattice
for $43 \times 96 = 4128$ is shown at
the right.

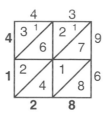

Legs of a Right Triangle (URG Unit 15; SG Unit 15)
The two sides of a right triangle that form the right angle.

Length of a Rectangle (URG Unit 4 & Unit 15;
SG Unit 4 & Unit 15)
The distance along one side of a rectangle.

Line
A set of points that form a straight path extending infi-
nitely in two directions.

Line of Reflection (URG Unit 10)
A line that acts as a mirror so that after a shape is flipped
over the line, corresponding points are at the same distance (equidistant) from the line.

Line Segment (URG Unit 14)
A part of a line between and including two points, called
the endpoints.

Liter (URG Unit 13)
Metric unit used to measure volume. A liter is a little
more than a quart.

Lowest Terms (SG Unit 11)
A fraction is in lowest terms if the numerator and
denominator have no common factor greater than 1.

M

Manipulated Variable (URG Unit 4; SG Unit 4)
In an experiment, the variable with values known at the
beginning of the experiment. The experimenter often
chooses these values before data is collected. The manipulated variable is often called the independent variable.

Mass (URG Unit 13)
The amount of matter in an object.

Mean (URG Unit 1 & Unit 4; SG Unit 1 & Unit 4)
An average of a set of numbers that is found by adding
the values of the data and dividing by the number of
values.

Measurement Division (URG Unit 4)
Division as equal grouping. The total number of objects
and the number of objects in each group are known. The
number of groups is the unknown. For example, tulip
bulbs come in packages of 8. If 216 bulbs are sold, how
many packages are sold?

Median (URG Unit 1; SG Unit 1)
For a set with an odd number of data arranged in order,
it is the middle number. For an even number of data
arranged in order, it is the mean of the two middle
numbers.

Meniscus (URG Unit 13)
The curved surface formed when a liquid creeps up the
side of a container (for example, a graduated cylinder).

Milliliter (ml) (URG Unit 13)
A measure of capacity in the metric system that is the
volume of a cube that is one centimeter long on each
side.

Mixed Number (URG Unit 3; SG Unit 3)
A number that is written as a whole number followed by
a fraction. It is equal to the sum of the whole number and
the fraction.

Mode (URG Unit 1; SG Unit 1)
The most common value in a data set.

Mr. Origin (URG Unit 10; SG Unit 10)
A plastic figure used to represent the origin of a coordinate system and to indicate the directions of the x- and
y- axes. (and possibly the z-axis).

N

N-gon (URG Unit 6; SG Unit 6)
A polygon with N sides.

Negative Number (URG Unit 10; SG Unit 10)
A number less than zero; a number to the left of zero on a
horizontal number line.

Nonagon (URG Unit 6; SG Unit 6)
A nine-sided polygon.

Numerator (URG Unit 3; SG Unit 3)
The number written above the line in a fraction. For
example, the 2 is the numerator in the fraction $\frac{2}{5}$. In this
case, we are interested in two of the five parts. (*See also*
denominator.)

Numerical Expression (URG Unit 4; SG Unit 4)
A combination of numbers and operations, e.g.,
$5 + 8 \div 4$.

Numerical Variable (URG Unit 1; SG Unit 1)
Variables with values that are numbers. (*See also* variable
and value.)

O

Obtuse Angle (URG Unit 6; SG Unit 6)
An angle that measures more than 90°.

Obtuse Triangle (URG Unit 6 & Unit 15; SG Unit 6 & Unit 15)
A triangle that has an obtuse angle.

Octagon (URG Unit 6; SG Unit 6)
An eight-sided polygon.

Ordered Pair (URG Unit 10; SG Unit 10)
A pair of numbers that gives the coordinates of a point on a grid in relation to the origin. The horizontal coordinate is given first; the vertical coordinate is given second. For example, the ordered pair (5, 3) gives the coordinates of the point that is 5 units to the right of the origin and 3 units up.

Origin (URG Unit 10; SG Unit 10)
The point at which the *x*- and *y*-axes intersect on a coordinate plane. The origin is described by the ordered pair (0, 0) and serves as a reference point so that all the points on the plane can be located by ordered pairs.

P

Pack (URG Unit 2; SG Unit 2)
A cube that measures 10 cm on each edge. It is one of the base-ten pieces and is often used to represent 1000. (*See also* base-ten pieces.)

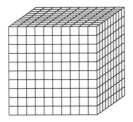

Parallel Lines (URG Unit 6 & Unit 10)
Lines that are in the same direction. In the plane, parallel lines are lines that do not intersect.

Parallelogram (URG Unit 6)
A quadrilateral with two pairs of parallel sides.

Partial Product (URG Unit 2)
One portion of the multiplication process in the all-partials multiplication method, e.g., in the problem 3 × 186 there are three partial products: 3 × 6 = 18, 3 × 80 = 240, and 3 × 100 = 300. (*See also* all-partials multiplication method.)

Partitive Division (URG Unit 4)
Division as equal sharing. The total number of objects and the number of groups are known. The number of objects in each group is the unknown. For example, Frank has 144 marbles that he divides equally into 6 groups. How many marbles are in each group?

Pentagon (URG Unit 6; SG Unit 6)
A five-sided polygon.

Percent (URG Unit 7; SG Unit 7)
Per hundred or out of 100. A special ratio that compares a number to 100. For example, 20% (twenty percent) of the jelly beans are yellow means that out of every 100 jelly beans, 20 are yellow.

Perimeter (URG Unit 15; SG Unit 15)
The distance around a two-dimensional shape.

Period (SG Unit 2)
A group of three places in a large number, starting on the right, often separated by commas as shown at the right.

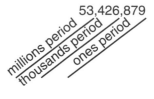

Perpendicular Lines (URG Unit 14 & Unit 15; SG Unit 14)
Lines that meet at right angles.

Pi (π) (URG Unit 14; SG Unit 14)
The ratio of the circumference to diameter of a circle. π = 3.14159265358979. . . . It is a nonterminating, nonrepeating decimal.

Place (SG Unit 2)
The position of a digit in a number.

Place Value (URG Unit 2; SG Unit 2)
The value of a digit in a number. For example, the 5 is in the hundreds place in 4573, so it stands for 500.

Polygon (URG Unit 6; SG Unit 6)
A two-dimensional connected figure made of line segments in which each endpoint of every side meets with an endpoint of exactly one other side.

Population (URG Unit 1 Unit 1)
A collection of persons or things whose properties will be analyzed in a survey or experiment.

Portfolio (URG Unit 2; SG Unit 2)
A collection of student work that show how a student's skills, attitudes, and knowledge change over time.

Positive Number (URG Unit 10; SG Unit 10)
A number greater than zero; a number to the right of zero on a horizontal number line.

Power (URG Unit 2; SG Unit 2)
An exponent. Read 10^4 as, "ten to the fourth power" or "ten to the fourth." We say 10,000 or 10^4 is the fourth power of ten.

Prime Factorization (URG Unit 11; SG Unit 11)
Writing a number as a product of primes. The prime factorization of 100 is 2 × 2 × 5 × 5.

Prime Number (URG Unit 11; SG Unit 11)
A number that has exactly two factors: itself and 1. For example, 7 has exactly two distinct factors, 1 and 7.

Probability (URG Unit 7; SG Unit 1 & Unit 7)
A number from 0 to 1 (0% to 100%) that describes how likely an event is to happen. The closer that the probability of an event is to one, the more likely the event will happen.

Product (URG Unit 2; SG Unit 2)
The answer to a multiplication problem. In the problem $3 \times 4 = 12$, 12 is the product.

Proper Fraction (URG Unit 3; SG Unit 3)
A fraction in which the numerator is less than the denominator. Proper fractions are less than one.

Proportion (URG Unit 3 & Unit 13; SG Unit 13)
A statement that two ratios are equal.

Protractor (URG Unit 6; SG Unit 6)
A tool for measuring angles.

Q

Quadrants (URG Unit 10; SG Unit 10)
The four sections of a coordinate grid that are separated by the axes.

Quadrilateral (URG Unit 6; SG Unit 6)
A polygon with four sides. (*See also* polygon.)

Quotient (URG Unit 4 & Unit 9; SG Unit 2, Unit 4, & Unit 9)
The answer to a division problem. In the problem $12 \div 3 = 4$, the 4 is the quotient.

R

Radius (URG Unit 14; SG Unit 14)
1. A line segment connecting the center of a circle to any point on the circle.
2. The length of this line segment.

Ratio (URG Unit 3 & Unit 12; SG Unit 3 & Unit 13)
A way to compare two numbers or quantities using division. It is often written as a fraction.

Ray (URG Unit 6; SG Unit 6)
A part of a line with one endpoint that extends indefinitely in one direction.

Rectangle (URG Unit 6; SG Unit 6)
A quadrilateral with four right angles.

Reflection (URG Unit 10)
(*See* flip.)

Regular Polygon (URG Unit 6; SG Unit 6; DAB Unit 6)
A polygon with all sides of equal length and all angles equal.

Remainder (URG Unit 4 & Unit 9; SG Unit 4 & Unit 9)
Something that remains or is left after a division problem. The portion of the dividend that is not evenly divisible by the divisor, e.g., $16 \div 5 = 3$ with 1 as a remainder.

Repeating Decimals (SG Unit 9)
A decimal fraction with one or more digits repeating without end.

Responding Variable (URG Unit 4; SG Unit 4)
The variable whose values result from the experiment. Experimenters find the values of the responding variable by doing the experiment. The responding variable is often called the dependent variable.

Rhombus (URG Unit 6; SG Unit 6)
A quadrilateral with four equal sides.

Right Angle (URG Unit 6; SG Unit 6)
An angle that measures 90°.

Right Triangle (URG Unit 6 & Unit 15; SG Unit 6 & Unit 15)
A triangle that contains a right angle.

Rubric (URG Unit 1)
A scoring guide that can be used to guide or assess student work.

S

Sample (URG Unit 1)
A part or subset of a population.

Scalene Triangle (URG Unit 15)
A triangle that has no sides that are equal in length.

Scientific Notation (URG Unit 2; SG Unit 2)
A way of writing numbers, particularly very large or very small numbers. A number in scientific notation has two factors. The first factor is a number greater than or equal to one and less than ten. The second factor is a power of 10 written with an exponent. For example, 93,000,000 written in scientific notation is 9.3×10^7.

Septagon (URG Unit 6; SG Unit 6)
A seven-sided polygon.

Side-Angle-Side (URG Unit 6 & Unit 14)
A geometric property stating that two triangles having two corresponding sides with the included angle equal are congruent.

Side-Side-Side (URG Unit 6)
A geometric property stating that two triangles having corresponding sides equal are congruent.

Sides of an Angle (URG Unit 6; SG Unit 6)
The sides of an angle are two rays with the same endpoint. (*See also* endpoint and ray.)

Sieve of Eratosthenes (SG Unit 11)
A method for separating prime numbers from nonprime numbers developed by Eratosthenes, an Egyptian librarian, in about 240 BCE.

Similar (URG Unit 6; SG Unit 6)
Similar shapes have the same shape but not necessarily the same size.

Skinny (URG Unit 2; SG Unit 2)
A block that measures 1 cm × 1 cm × 10 cm.
It is one of the base-ten pieces
and is often used to represent 10.
(*See also* base-ten pieces.)

Slide (URG Unit 10; SG Unit 10)
Moving a geometric figure in the plane by moving every point of the figure the same distance in the same direction. Also called translation.

Speed (URG Unit 3 & Unit 5; SG Unit 3 & Unit 5)
The ratio of distance moved to time taken, e.g.,
3 miles/1 hour or 3 mph is a speed.

Square (URG Unit 6 & Unit 14; SG Unit 6)
A quadrilateral with four equal sides and four right angles.

Square Centimeter (URG Unit 4; SG Unit 4)
The area of a square that is 1 cm long on each side.

Square Number (URG Unit 11)
A number that is the product of a whole number multiplied by itself. For example, 25 is a square number since 5 × 5 = 25. A square number can be represented by a square array with the same number of rows as columns. A square array for 25 has 5 rows of 5 objects in each row or 25 total objects.

Standard Form (SG Unit 2)
The traditional way to write a number, e.g., standard form for three hundred fifty-seven is 357. (*See also* expanded form and word form.)

Standard Units (URG Unit 4)
Internationally or nationally agreed-upon units used in measuring variables, e.g., centimeters and inches are standard units used to measure length and square centimeters and square inches are used to measure area.

Straight Angle (URG Unit 6; SG Unit 6)
An angle that measures 180°.

T

Ten Percent (URG Unit 4; SG Unit 4)
10 out of every hundred or $\frac{1}{10}$.

Tessellation (URG Unit 6 & Unit 10; SG Unit 6)
A pattern made up of one or more repeated shapes that completely covers a surface without any gaps or overlaps.

Translation
(*See* slide.)

Trapezoid (URG Unit 6)
A quadrilateral with exactly one pair of parallel sides.

Triangle (URG Unit 6; SG Unit 6)
A polygon with three sides.

Triangulating (URG Unit 6; SG Unit 6)
Partitioning a polygon into two or more nonoverlapping triangles by drawing diagonals that do not intersect.

Turn-Around Facts (URG Unit 2)
Multiplication facts that have the same factors but in a different order, e.g., 3 × 4 = 12 and 4 × 3 = 12. (*See also* commutative property of multiplication.)

Twin Primes (URG Unit 11; SG Unit 11)
A pair of prime numbers whose difference is 2. For example, 3 and 5 are twin primes.

U

Unit Ratio (URG Unit 13; SG Unit 13)
A ratio with a denominator of one.

V

Value (URG Unit 1; SG Unit 1)
The possible outcomes of a variable. For example, red, green, and blue are possible values for the variable *color*. Two meters and 1.65 meters are possible values for the variable *length*.

Variable (URG Unit 1; SG Unit 1)
1. An attribute or quantity that changes or varies. (*See also* categorical variable and numerical variable.)
2. A symbol that can stand for a variable.

Variables in Proportion (URG Unit 13; SG Unit 13)
When the ratio of two variables in an experiment is always the same, the variables are in proportion.

Velocity (URG Unit 5; SG Unit 5)
Speed in a given direction. Speed is the ratio of the distance traveled to time taken.

Vertex (URG Unit 6; SG Unit 6)
A common point of two rays or line segments that form an angle.

Volume (URG Unit 13)
The measure of the amount of space occupied by an object.

W

Whole Number
Any of the numbers 0, 1, 2, 3, 4, 5, 6 and so on.

Width of a Rectangle (URG Unit 4 & Unit 15; SG Unit 4 & Unit 15)
The distance along one side of a rectangle is the length and the distance along an adjacent side is the width.

Word Form (SG Unit 2)
A number expressed in words, e.g., the word form for 123 is "one hundred twenty-three." (*See also* expanded form and standard form.)

X

Y

Z